World Peace

Other Books of Related Interest

Opposing Viewpoints Series

Domestic Terrorism

North and South Korea

Religious Liberties

US Foreign Policy

At Issue Series

Biological and Chemical Weapons

Drones

Guns and Crime

Is Society Becoming Less Civil?

Current Controversies Series

Developing Nations

Espionage and Intelligence

Immigration

Politics and Religion

"Congress shall make
no law . . . abridging
the freedom of speech,
or of the press."

First Amendment to the US Constitution

The basic foundation of our democracy is the First Amendment guarantee of freedom of expression. The Opposing Viewpoints series is dedicated to the concept of this basic freedom and the idea that it is more important to practice it than to enshrine it.

World Peace

Margaret Haerens, Book Editor

GREENHAVEN PRESS
A part of Gale, Cengage Learning

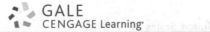

Farmington Hills, Mich • San Francisco • New York • Waterville, Maine
Meriden, Conn • Mason, Ohio • Chicago

Patricia Coryell, *Vice President & Publisher, New Products & GVRL*
Douglas Dentino, *Manager, New Products*
Judy Galens, *Acquisitions Editor*

Articles in Greenhaven Press anthologies are often edited for length to meet page requirements. In addition, original titles of these works are changed to clearly present the main thesis and to explicitly indicate the author's opinion. Every effort is made to ensure that Greenhaven Press accurately reflects the original intent of the authors. Every effort has been made to trace the owners of copyrighted material.

Cover Image copyright © pashabo/Shutterstock.com.

LIBRARY OF CONGRESS CATALOGING-IN-PUBLICATION DATA

World peace / edited by Margaret Haerens.
        pages cm. -- (Opposing viewpoints)
    Includes bibliographical references and index.
        ISBN 978-0-7377-7304-0 (hardback) -- ISBN 978-0-7377-7305-7 (paperback)
    1. Peace--Juvenile literature. I. Haerens, Margaret.
    JZ5538.W78 2015
    327.1'72--dc23

                                                                    2014040681

Printed in the United States of America
1 2 3 4 5 6 7 19 18 17 16 15

Contents

Chapter 3: What Economic, Social, and Political Factors May Lead to World Peace?

Chapter 4: What Are the Greatest Threats to World Peace?

Why Consider Opposing Viewpoints?

> *"The only way in which a human being can make some approach to knowing the whole of a subject is by hearing what can be said about it by persons of every variety of opinion and studying all modes in which it can be looked at by every character of mind. No wise man ever acquired his wisdom in any mode but this."*
>
> *John Stuart Mill*

In our media-intensive culture it is not difficult to find differing opinions. Thousands of newspapers and magazines and dozens of radio and television talk shows resound with differing points of view. The difficulty lies in deciding which opinion to agree with and which "experts" seem the most credible. The more inundated we become with differing opinions and claims, the more essential it is to hone critical reading and thinking skills to evaluate these ideas. Opposing Viewpoints books address this problem directly by presenting stimulating debates that can be used to enhance and teach these skills. The varied opinions contained in each book examine many different aspects of a single issue. While examining these conveniently edited opposing views, readers can develop critical thinking skills such as the ability to compare and contrast authors' credibility, facts, argumentation styles, use of persuasive techniques, and other stylistic tools. In short, the Opposing Viewpoints Series is an ideal way to attain the higher-level thinking and reading skills so essential in a culture of diverse and contradictory opinions.

In addition to providing a tool for critical thinking, Opposing Viewpoints books challenge readers to question their own strongly held opinions and assumptions. Most people form their opinions on the basis of upbringing, peer pressure, and personal, cultural, or professional bias. By reading carefully balanced opposing views, readers must directly confront new ideas as well as the opinions of those with whom they disagree. This is not to argue simplistically that everyone who reads opposing views will—or should—change his or her opinion. Instead, the series enhances readers' understanding of their own views by encouraging confrontation with opposing ideas. Careful examination of others' views can lead to the readers' understanding of the logical inconsistencies in their own opinions, perspective on why they hold an opinion, and the consideration of the possibility that their opinion requires further evaluation.

Evaluating Other Opinions

To ensure that this type of examination occurs, Opposing Viewpoints books present all types of opinions. Prominent spokespeople on different sides of each issue as well as well-known professionals from many disciplines challenge the reader. An additional goal of the series is to provide a forum for other, less known, or even unpopular viewpoints. The opinion of an ordinary person who has had to make the decision to cut off life support from a terminally ill relative, for example, may be just as valuable and provide just as much insight as a medical ethicist's professional opinion. The editors have two additional purposes in including these less known views. One, the editors encourage readers to respect others' opinions—even when not enhanced by professional credibility. It is only by reading or listening to and objectively evaluating others' ideas that one can determine whether they are worthy of consideration. Two, the inclusion of such viewpoints encourages the important critical thinking skill of objectively evaluating an author's credentials and bias. This evaluation will illuminate an author's reasons for taking a particular stance on an issue and will aid in readers' evaluation of the author's ideas.

It is our hope that these books will give readers a deeper understanding of the issues debated and an appreciation of the complexity of even seemingly simple issues when good and honest people disagree. This awareness is particularly important in a democratic society such as ours in which people enter into public debate to determine the common good. Those with whom one disagrees should not be regarded as enemies but rather as people whose views deserve careful examination and may shed light on one's own.

Thomas Jefferson once said that "difference of opinion leads to inquiry, and inquiry to truth." Jefferson, a broadly educated man, argued that "if a nation expects to be ignorant and free . . . it expects what never was and never will be." As individuals and as a nation, it is imperative that we consider the opinions of others and examine them with skill and discernment. The Opposing Viewpoints series is intended to help readers achieve this goal.

David L. Bender and Bruno Leone,
Founders

Introduction

On June 12, 2014, three Israeli teenagers were abducted while hitchhiking to their homes in the West Bank, a Palestinian territory controlled by its neighbor, Israel. Immediately, suspicion fell on Hamas, an Islamist political organization and militant group, as the perpetrator. Widely considered a terrorist outfit, Hamas was formed in 1987 for the purpose of eliminating Israel's hold on the Palestinian territories, which include the West Bank and Gaza Strip, through violent means. It was assumed that the three young men had been unfortunate victims of the ongoing bloody conflict between Hamas and Israel.

Hamas denied any involvement in the kidnappings, but the Israel Defense Forces (IDF) launched a search mission, named Operation Brother's Keeper, for the three teenagers. Within days of the incident, hundreds of Palestinians were questioned and arrested. Many of those imprisoned were Hamas leaders. Operation Brother's Keeper was the most severe crackdown on Hamas by Israel in over a decade.

On June 30, the bodies of the three teenagers were found near the city of Hebron. Israeli prime minister Benjamin Netanyahu blamed Hamas for the deaths, promising that the group would pay for the crime. "Hamas is responsible," he stated at the funeral of the young men. "Hamas will pay, and Hamas will continue to pay."

However, many in the intelligence community considered it unlikely that Hamas was behind the brutal crime. Instead, intelligence authorities began to believe that the murders were the work of a rogue cell, a few Palestinian extremists loosely associated with Hamas but not under the group's control.

Tension between Palestinians in the West Bank and Israeli forces escalated in the days after the funeral. On July 2, a seventeen-year-old Palestinian, Mohammed Abu Khdeir, was abducted and killed, his body found badly burned. The preliminary evidence suggested that it was an attack carried out by right-wing Jewish extremists as revenge for the killing of the three kidnapped teenagers. On July 6, Israeli police arrested and charged three Israeli men for the murder of Khdeir after they confessed.

Despite the efforts of Israeli authorities to deal with the repercussions of the rigorous crackdown on Hamas and Khdeir's murder, violent clashes between Palestinians and Israeli forces continued to escalate. Fierce riots raged in several areas of Gaza and the West Bank. As Palestinian anger built after Khdeir's mutilated body was found, Arab militants in Gaza launched rocket attacks at several Israeli cities. Many of these attacks were thwarted by the Iron Dome, a self-defense system that intercepted Hamas rockets before they reached the ground. In response to the frequent rocket attacks, the IDF launched its own strikes at Hamas targets, killing several militants as well as civilians.

Palestinian president Mahmoud Abbas addressed the escalating crisis by urging Hamas to stop its shelling of Israel from Gaza. "What are you trying to achieve by sending rockets?" he asked in a televised address on Palestine TV. "We prefer to fight with wisdom and politics."

On July 8, the IDF launched Operation Protective Edge, a military offensive against Hamas in Gaza with the objective of putting an end to the militant group's constant rocket attacks on Israel. Israeli forces invaded Gaza on July 15 in order to dismantle infrastructure used by Gaza, particularly an elaborate set of underground tunnels that connect Gaza to Israel. Hamas militants used the tunnel to store weapons and launch raids on Israeli targets.

As Palestinian civilian casualties began to mount, international pressure began to intensify for a cease-fire in order to negotiate a diplomatic solution to the ongoing conflict. As of August 4, the United Nations had estimated that more than seventeen hundred Palestinians had been killed, the overwhelming majority of them civilians. Televised coverage of the rising death toll, which included footage of the aftermath of Israeli bombings and the recovery of the bodies of women and children, prompted denunciations from around the world.

"How many more deaths must there be to stop what must be called the carnage in Gaza?" asked French foreign minister Laurent Fabius. "The tradition of friendship between France and Israel is old and Israel's right to security is total, but this right does not justify the killing of children and the massacre of civilians."

On its part, Israel denied targeting civilians and argued that Hamas was to blame for civilian deaths because it often places military targets, such as weapon caches and rocket launchers, in hospitals, schools, or humanitarian shelters. In many cases, Israeli authorities also warned civilians to evacuate certain areas in anticipation of a military attack in order to prevent injuries and casualties. Despite these efforts, the death toll in Gaza continued to rise.

Observers worried that the conflict could spread and draw in neighboring states, many of which have been hostile toward Israel and supportive of the Palestinians and Hamas, and eventually destabilize the entire region. By the end of summer, the negotiation of a lasting cease-fire became a top priority for the international community, even if a long-term solution remained frustratingly out of reach.

For decades, the Israeli-Palestinian conflict has been viewed as a serious threat to world peace. The authors of the viewpoints in *Opposing Viewpoints: World Peace* examine such threats to world peace in chapters titled "How Should World Peace Be Regarded?," "How Can World Peace Be Established?," "What Economic, Social, and Political Factors May Lead to World Peace?," and "What Are the Greatest Threats to World Peace?" The information found in this volume provides insight into the feasibility of attaining world peace, various obstacles to it, and the role of the United States in facilitating global harmony.

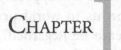

CHAPTER 1

How Should World Peace Be Regarded?

Chapter Preface

Today's world is a violent place. Bloody civil wars rage in Iraq, Syria, Ukraine, and South Sudan. In a number of places around the world, sectarian conflict kills thousands of people and displaces millions. Mass shootings cut down hundreds of people every year; just in America alone, more than nine hundred people were slaughtered by mass shooters over the past seven years. Organized crime, particularly drug cartels, has wreaked havoc in Central and South America. Reports of brutal and shocking violence appear every day in newspapers around the globe.

Despite the steady stream of stories on these horrible conflicts and violence, some experts believe that the world is becoming a more peaceful place. They point to statistics that show that there have been steep declines in deaths from war, homicides, sectarian violence, and family violence. For example, in the Middle Ages, battlefield deaths averaged more than five hundred out of every one hundred thousand people. By nineteenth-century France, the average dropped to seventy people. Today, it is estimated that battlefield deaths have declined to less than one person per one hundred thousand people.

According to criminologist Manuel Eisner, who studied the prevalence of Western European homicides from the thirteenth century to the end of the twentieth century, murder rates have also dropped sharply. In an examination of England's murder rate throughout this time period, Eisner notes that the rate plummeted from twenty-four murders out of every one hundred thousand people in the fourteenth century to 0.6 per every one hundred thousand in the twentieth century.

Harvard University psychologist Steven Pinker is one of the leading voices on the evolution of violence in society. He argues that we are living in the most peaceful era in human history, attributing humankind's peaceful evolution to higher intelligence. As humans become smarter generation after generation, war and other forms of violence become a less reasonable way to settle disputes or to deal with other communities. "As we get smarter, we try to think of better ways of getting everyone to turn their swords into ploughshares at the same time," Pinker said in a recent *Huffington Post* interview. "Human life has become more precious than it used to be."

Other factors that have been cited as reasons for the more peaceful state of today's world are the spread of democratic governments; the success of international security organizations, economic development programs, and nongovernmental organizations; and cultural and societal shifts, including the empowerment of women and religious and ethnic tolerance in some parts of the world.

For some security analysts, however, there are still areas of concern. They argue that although wars and large-scale conflicts may be on the decline, there is a rise in other types of conflict. According to a 2014 Institute for Economics and Peace report, rates of domestic terrorism in many parts of the world have risen since the start of the Iraq war in 2003. In the past several years, internal conflict within nations has increased, signaling political instability in a number of regions, including the Middle East, parts of Africa, and the Balkans.

The question of whether the present-day world is more peaceful is one of the topics examined in the following chapter, which explores various ways to think about world peace. Other viewpoints address the role of world peace in international security circles and the possibility of attaining global harmony.

| "When people come to deeply believe in notions that promote peace, peace will follow like a shadow follows the body."

World Peace Is Possible

Alex Lickerman

Alex Lickerman is a physician, author, and assistant vice president for Student Health and Counseling Services at the University of Chicago. In the following viewpoint, he contends that world peace is possible if enough people seek to transform themselves and learn to control the negative aspects of their human nature. If large numbers of people become experts at living—which means attaining a level of wisdom, self-discipline, and joy—conflicts would naturally decrease and enlightened world leaders would be more focused on solving the problems that often lead to war. Lickerman concedes that such a massive global transformation would be a long-term project, but even the most ambitious goals must start with the individual. He urges people to have the courage to start their own journeys toward self-enlightenment and become true experts at living.

As you read, consider the following questions:

1. Where does the author believe the true cause of war lies?

2. According to Lickerman, what did the original Buddha, Shakyamuni, say about killing?

3. What is the ultimate dream of every Nichiren Buddhist, according to the author?

When I was in grammar school learning about World War II, I remember thinking how grateful I was that society had finally matured to the point in the intervening years that war no longer ever broke out. Today I can hardly remember what bizarre thought process led me to conclude that people had actually become less barbaric with time. I do remember I also believed racial prejudice had died out decades ago and that the pronouncement of guilt or innocence by our justice system reflected actual guilt or innocence.

But I've forgiven my earlier self this embarrassing naïveté because I think his conclusions weren't based entirely on ignorance as much as on a hope for how things could be. And though for many years I scoffed at the notion, I have to confess now that I've become convinced world peace is indeed possible.

What Is the True Cause of War?

Countries don't go to war. The *leaders* of countries go to war. They marshal their reasons, stir up the public, dehumanize the enemy (as I wrote about in an earlier post, "The True Cause of Cruelty"), and send out their forces. The number of people actually responsible for the decision to go to war can usually fit comfortably inside a single large-sized room.

Leaders, of course, only occasionally represent the best of what humanity has to offer so they usually exhibit the same failings and weaknesses as the rest of us. They get angry when they shouldn't, let their egos motivate them more than they should, and are entirely too concerned with doing what's popular rather than what's right. They suffer from the same three poisons as the populations they lead: greed, anger, and stupidity.

The true cause of war lies in the unchecked rampaging of these three poisons through the hearts of individual people. Though the situations confronting world leaders that lead them to decide to wage war often seem complex, the only way in which they're different from conflict that erupts between two people standing in a room is that they occur on a larger scale. But if in civilized societies we expect people to work out their differences amicably (whether themselves or with the help of the courts), why don't those same expectations apply to differences between civilized countries?

Is War Ever Necessary?

In a world in which tyrannies continue to exist, war may in fact sometimes be justified. In the same way it's necessary to fight to defend oneself when attacked, so too it's sometimes necessary to go to war to put down injustice, or even the possibility of injustice when its likelihood is great enough. Rarely, however, is this given as a primary reason. Even democracies seem to be roused to war only by self-interest.

Fair enough. But when any leader chooses war, *he or she should do so with a heavy heart*. As the original Buddha, Shakyamuni, once said when asked if killing was ever to be permitted: "It is enough to kill the will to kill." In other words, we should strive to kill the *idea* that killing others should be anything other than the very last action we ever permit ourselves to take. Shakyamuni was a realist. He knew the world would always be filled with people bent on committing evil, people whose ideas about how to live involved oppressing and killing others, and though he felt compassion even for them would speak loudly and passionately about the necessity of standing against them in concrete, practical ways.

Expert Human Beings

To achieve world peace—to create a world in which war ceases to break out—seems impossible because of the sheer number of people who haven't yet mastered themselves, who haven't tamed their ambition to raise themselves up at the expense of others, and who haven't learned to start from today onward, letting past wrongs committed by both sides remain in the past. In short, it seems an impossible dream because we're in desperately short supply of human beings who are *experts at living.*

An expert at living isn't a person who never experiences greed, anger, or stupidity but rather one who remains in firm control of those negative parts (which can never be entirely eliminated), who's able to surmount his or her darkest negativity, and displays a *peerless ability to resolve conflict peacefully.* What generates this expert ability to resolve conflict? Wisdom and joy. Wise people are happy people, and happy people are wise. If enough people in the world's population became happy and wise, violence would be used far less often to solve conflict. If this pool of experts at living became large enough, we'd start seeing some of our leaders being picked from among them. And if enough leaders were experts at living, war, too, would be used far less often to solve conflict and further the interests of nations.

I'm no Pollyanna. I fully recognize that as long as there remain inequities between classes, as long as people feel they have little hope for a good life and remain unable to tolerate others believing differently than they do about important issues, violence and war will continue. Which means the real path to world peace can't be found in the passing of more laws, in diplomacy, or even in war itself. It can only be found in the actions individual human beings take to reform the tenets they hold in their hearts in order to become experts at living. Some argue human nature being what it is precludes the possibility of world peace, but I would counter that hu-

"HOW COME THERE AREN'T ANY PEACE HEROES?"

© Harley Schwardron/Cartoonstock.com.

man nature doesn't need to change—it only needs to be managed. Haven't countless numbers of us already learned to do this every day, denying our baser impulses in order to contribute to solutions instead of problems?

The Real Barrier to World Peace

The reason most scoff at the notion of achieving world peace is because if you buy the principle that individual human revolution is the real solution, then literally some *billions* of people would need to actively embrace the notion of devoting themselves to continual self-reformation. But—if you buy the principle that enough people becoming experts at living would create world peace, then you can't argue world peace is literally impossible—just extraordinarily unlikely.

I don't believe world peace will be achieved in my lifetime. But I do believe it won't be achieved in any lifetime after mine unless I make causes for it to happen now. How can I—and you—make those causes? As [Mahatma] Gandhi famously said, by becoming the change we wish to see. Strive to become an expert at living. Be good to those around you in concrete ways. Create an island of peace in your own life. If you do, it will spread. If enough of us do this, our islands will meet, ceasing to be islands and becoming whole continents. World peace exists literally in the actions each one of [us] takes in our own lives.

The most significant obstacle to achieving world peace isn't the extraordinary difficulty involved in becoming a genuine expert at living, though. It's that those most in need of re-forming the tenets they hold in their hearts, who most need training in how to be an expert at living, *are those least interested in it.* . . .

The only real lever we have to pull with such people is their desire to become happy. We must convince them to follow our lead by becoming so happy ourselves—so ridiculously, genuinely happy—that they decide on their own they want to be like us, that they want what we have. And then we have to show them how to get it. Good ideas are our weapons. When people come to deeply believe in notions that promote peace, peace will follow like a shadow follows the body.

To say this strategy is long term would be an understatement. But all other solutions seem to me even less likely to succeed than the one I'm proposing here. You may think of me as hopelessly naïve as my younger self who thought war had already been eliminated for continuing to hope that widespread, lasting peace is possible, but as John Lennon famously sang, I'm not the only one. The ultimate dream of every Nichiren Buddhist is the accomplishment of world peace by the achievement of individual happiness.

We need to summon the courage to even voice a commitment to the goal. We can't worry about if it can be done at all, or how long it might take. It can be done. It will take a long, long time. But the argument that it *can't* be done and therefore shouldn't be attempted is the argument of cowards. If there weren't people throughout our history who refused to listen to that logic, we'd all still be living in caves. Look again at the last word in the title of this post.

> "Even if we do not achieve perfect peace
> on earth, because perfect peace is not of
> this earth, common endeavours to gain
> peace will unite individuals and na-
> tions in trust and friendship and help
> to make our human community safer
> and kinder."

World Peace Is a Worthwhile but Unattainable Goal

Aung San Suu Kyi

Aung San Suu Kyi is a human rights activist, politician, and the recipient of the 1991 Nobel Peace Prize. In the following viewpoint, she reflects on the years she spent under house arrest for her political activism in Burma. She says the support of the international community is key to creating a more peaceful, prosperous, and secure Burma. Absolute peace, whether in Burma or in the world, is unattainable; in her opinion, there are negative forces in society and those forces can never be removed. They can be mitigated, however, in order to optimize the potential of every country to be a kinder and more peaceful environment. She says it is important to realize that this global effort to create a more

Aung San Suu Kyi, "Nobel Lecture," Nobelprize.org, June 16, 2012. Copyright © 2012 by Nobelprize.org. All rights reserved. Reproduced by permission.

peaceful society brings the people of the world together, allowing them to form bonds and recognize common goals—the most important of these goals is a world in which every individual has the right to live in peace and fulfill his or her potential.

As you read, consider the following questions:

1. How did Aung San Suu Kyi learn that she had been awarded the 1991 Nobel Peace Prize?

2. What era of poetry holds a special significance for the author?

3. According to the author, what year did Burma achieve its independence?

Long years ago, sometimes it seems many lives ago, I was at Oxford listening to the radio programme *Desert Island Discs* with my young son Alexander. It was a well-known programme (for all I know it still continues) on which famous people from all walks of life were invited to talk about the eight discs, the one book besides the bible and the complete works of Shakespeare, and the one luxury item they would wish to have with them were they to be marooned on a desert island. At the end of the programme, which we had both enjoyed, Alexander asked me if I thought I might ever be invited to speak on *Desert Island Discs*. "Why not?" I responded lightly. Since he knew that in general only celebrities took part in the programme he proceeded to ask, with genuine interest, for what reason I thought I might be invited. I considered this for a moment and then answered: "Perhaps because I'd have won the Nobel Prize for literature," and we both laughed. The prospect seemed pleasant but hardly probable.

(I cannot now remember why I gave that answer, perhaps because I had recently read a book by a Nobel laureate or perhaps because the *Desert Island* celebrity of that day had been a famous writer.)

In 1989, when my late husband Michael Aris came to see me during my first term of house arrest, he told me that a friend, John Finnis, had nominated me for the Nobel Peace Prize. This time also I laughed. For an instant Michael looked amazed, then he realized why I was amused. The Nobel Peace Prize? A pleasant prospect, but quite improbable! So how did I feel when I was actually awarded the Nobel Prize for peace? The question has been put to me many times and this is surely the most appropriate occasion on which to examine what the Nobel Prize means to me and what peace means to me.

A Personal Perspective on the Award

As I have said repeatedly in many an interview, I heard the news that I had been awarded the Nobel Peace Prize on the radio one evening. It did not altogether come as a surprise because I had been mentioned as one of the front-runners for the prize in a number of broadcasts during the previous week. While drafting this lecture, I have tried very hard to remember what my immediate reaction to the announcement of the award had been. I think, I can no longer be sure, it was something like: "Oh, so they've decided to give it to me." It did not seem quite real because in a sense I did not feel myself to be quite real at that time.

Often during my days of house arrest it felt as though I were no longer a part of the real world. There was the house which was my world, there was the world of others who also were not free but who were together in prison as a community, and there was the world of the free; each was a different planet pursuing its own separate course in an indifferent universe. What the Nobel Peace Prize did was to draw me once again into the world of other human beings outside the isolated area in which I lived, to restore a sense of reality to me. This did not happen instantly, of course, but as the days and months went by and news of reactions to the award came over the airwaves, I began to understand the significance of the Nobel Prize. It had made me real once again; it had drawn me back into the wider human community. And what was more important, the Nobel Prize had drawn the attention of the world to the struggle for democracy and human rights in Burma [also known as Myanmar]. We were not going to be forgotten.

To be forgotten. The French say that to part is to die a little. To be forgotten, too, is to die a little. It is to lose some of the links that anchor us to the rest of humanity. When I met Burmese migrant workers and refugees during my recent visit to Thailand, many cried out: "Don't forget us!" They meant: "don't forget our plight, don't forget to do what you can to help us, don't forget we also belong to your world." When the Nobel Committee awarded the Peace Prize to me they were recognizing that the oppressed and the isolated in Burma were also a part of the world, they were recognizing the oneness of humanity. So for me receiving the Nobel Peace Prize means personally extending my concerns for democracy and human rights beyond national borders. The Nobel Peace Prize opened up a door in my heart.

Peace in Burma

The Burmese concept of peace can be explained as the happiness arising from the cessation of factors that militate against the harmonious and the wholesome. The word *nyein-chan* translates literally as the beneficial coolness that comes when a fire is extinguished. Fires of suffering and strife are raging around the world. In my own country, hostilities have not ceased in the far north; to the west, communal violence resulting in arson and murder were taking place just several days before I started out on the journey that has brought me here today. News of atrocities in other reaches of the earth abound. Reports of hunger, disease, displacement, joblessness, poverty, injustice, discrimination, prejudice, bigotry; these are our daily fare. Everywhere there are negative forces eating away at the foundations of peace. Everywhere can be found thoughtless dissipation of material and human resources that are necessary for the conservation of harmony and happiness in our world.

The First World War represented a terrifying waste of youth and potential, a cruel squandering of the positive forces of our planet. The poetry of that era has a special significance for me because I first read it at a time when I was the same age as many of those young men who had to face the prospect of withering before they had barely blossomed. A young American fighting with the French Foreign Legion wrote before he was killed in action in 1916 that he would meet his death: "at some disputed barricade;" "on some scarred slope of battered hill;" "at midnight in some flaming town." Youth and love and life perishing forever in senseless attempts to capture nameless, unremembered places. And for what? Nearly a century on, we have yet to find a satisfactory answer.

Are we not still guilty, if to a less violent degree, of recklessness, of improvidence with regard to our future and our humanity? War is not the only arena where peace is done to death. Wherever suffering is ignored, there will be the seeds of conflict, for suffering degrades and embitters and enrages.

Six Great Sufferings

A positive aspect of living in isolation was that I had ample time in which to ruminate over the meaning of words and precepts that I had known and accepted all my life. As a Buddhist, I had heard about *dukha*, generally translated as suffering, since I was a small child. Almost on a daily basis elderly, and sometimes not so elderly, people around me would murmur "dukha, dukha" when they suffered from aches and pains or when they met with some small, annoying mishaps. However, it was only during my years of house arrest that I got around to investigating the nature of the six great dukha. These are: to be conceived, to age, to sicken, to die, to be parted from those one loves, to be forced to live in propinquity with those one does not love. I examined each of the six great sufferings, not in a religious context but in the context of our ordinary, everyday lives. If suffering were an unavoidable part of our existence, we should try to alleviate it as far as possible in practical, earthly ways. I mulled over the effectiveness of ante- and post-natal programmes and mother and child care; of adequate facilities for the aging population; of comprehensive health services; of compassionate nursing and hospices. I was particularly intrigued by the last two kinds of suffering: to be parted from those one loves and to be forced to live in propinquity with those one does not love. What experiences might our Lord Buddha have undergone in his own life that he had included these two states among the great sufferings? I thought of prisoners and refugees, of migrant workers and victims of human trafficking, of that great mass of the uprooted of the earth who have been torn away from their homes, parted from families and friends, forced to live out their lives among strangers who are not always welcoming.

We are fortunate to be living in an age when social welfare and humanitarian assistance are recognized not only as desirable but necessary. I am fortunate to be living in an age when the fate of prisoners of conscience anywhere has become the concern of peoples everywhere, an age when democracy and human rights are widely, even if not universally, accepted as the birthright of all. How often during my years under house arrest have I drawn strength from my favourite passages in the preamble to the Universal Declaration of Human Rights:

> ... disregard and contempt for human rights have resulted in barbarous acts which have outraged the conscience of mankind, and the advent of a world in which human beings shall enjoy freedom of speech and belief and freedom from fear and want has been proclaimed as the highest aspirations of the common people,

... it is essential, if man is not to be compelled to have re-course, as a last resort, to rebellion against tyranny and op-pression, that human rights should be protected by the rule of law ...

If I am asked why I am fighting for human rights in Burma the above passages will provide the answer. If I am asked why I am fighting for democracy in Burma, it is because I believe that democratic institutions and practices are necessary for the guarantee of human rights.

Cautious Optimism

Over the past year, there have been signs that the endeavours of those who believe in democracy and human rights are be-ginning to bear fruit in Burma. There have been changes in a positive direction; steps towards democratization have been taken. If I advocate cautious optimism it is not because I do not have faith in the future but because I do not want to en-courage blind faith. Without faith in the future, without the conviction that democratic values and fundamental human rights are not only necessary but possible for our society, our movement could not have been sustained throughout the de-stroying years. Some of our warriors fell at their post, some deserted us, but a dedicated core remained strong and com-mitted. At times when I think of the years that have passed, I am amazed that so many remained staunch under the most trying circumstances. Their faith in our cause is not blind; it is based on a clear-eyed assessment of their own powers of endurance and a profound respect for the aspirations of our people.

It is because of recent changes in my country that I am with you today; and these changes have come about because of you and other lovers of freedom and justice who contrib-uted towards a global awareness of our situation. Before con-tinuing to speak of my country, may I speak out for our pris-oners of conscience? There still remain such prisoners in

Burma. It is to be feared that because the best known detainees have been released, the remainder, the unknown ones, will be forgotten. I am standing here because I was once a prisoner of conscience. As you look at me and listen to me, please remember the often repeated truth that one prisoner of conscience is one too many. Those who have not yet been freed, those who have not yet been given access to the benefits of justice in my country number much more than one. Please remember them and do whatever is possible to affect their earliest, unconditional release.

Burma is a country of many ethnic nationalities, and faith in its future can be founded only on a true spirit of union. Since we achieved independence in 1948, there never has been a time when we could claim the whole country was at peace. We have not been able to develop the trust and understanding necessary to remove causes of conflict. Hopes were raised by cease-fires that were maintained from the early 1990s until 2010 when these broke down over the course of a few months. One unconsidered move can be enough to remove long-standing cease-fires. In recent months, negotiations between the government and ethnic nationality forces have been making progress. We hope that cease-fire agreements will lead to political settlements founded on the aspirations of the peoples and the spirit of union.

The Future of Burma

My party, the National League for Democracy, and I stand ready and willing to play any role in the process of national reconciliation. The reform measures that were put into motion by President U Thein Sein's government can be sustained only with the intelligent cooperation of all internal forces: the military, our ethnic nationalities, political parties, the media, civil society organizations, the business community and, most important of all, the general public. We can say that reform is effective only if the lives of the people are improved and in

Aung San Suu Kyi

In 1988 Aung San Suu Kyi (born 1945) became the pre-eminent leader in Burma (now Myanmar) of the movement toward the reestablishment of democracy in that state. In 1991, while under house arrest, she was awarded the Nobel Peace Prize. Suu Kyi was released from her most recent house arrest term on November 13, 2010.

Aung San Suu Kyi was internationally recognized as a vibrant symbol of resistance to authoritarian rule. On July 20, 1989, she was placed under house arrest by the military coup leaders, called the State Law and Order Restoration Council (SLORC), who came to power in Myanmar on September 18, 1988, in the wake of a popular but crushed uprising against the previous, and also military-headed, socialist government. The nation's name had been changed from Burma to Myanmar in 1980.

"Aung San Suu Kyi," Biography in Context.
Detroit, MI: Gale, 2014.

this regard, the international community has a vital role to play. Development and humanitarian aid, bilateral agreements and investments should be coordinated and calibrated to ensure that these will promote social, political and economic growth that is balanced and sustainable. The potential of our country is enormous. This should be nurtured and developed to create not just a more prosperous but also a more harmonious, democratic society where our people can live in peace, security and freedom.

The peace of our world is indivisible. As long as negative forces are getting the better of positive forces anywhere, we are all at risk. It may be questioned whether all negative forces could ever be removed. The simple answer is: "No!" It is in human nature to contain both the positive and the negative. However, it is also within human capability to work to reinforce the positive and to minimize or neutralize the negative. Absolute peace in our world is an unattainable goal.

But it is one towards which we must continue to journey, our eyes fixed on it as a traveller in a desert fixes his eyes on the one guiding star that will lead him to salvation. Even if we do not achieve perfect peace on earth, because perfect peace is not of this earth, common endeavours to gain peace will unite individuals and nations in trust and friendship and help to make our human community safer and kinder.

The Lesson of Kindness

I used the word 'kinder' after careful deliberation; I might say the careful deliberation of many years. Of the sweets of adversity, and let me say that these are not numerous, I have found the sweetest, the most precious of all, is the lesson I learnt on the value of kindness. Every kindness I received, small or big, convinced me that there could never be enough of it in our world. To be kind is to respond with sensitivity and human warmth to the hopes and needs of others. Even the briefest touch of kindness can lighten a heavy heart. Kindness can change the lives of people. Norway has shown exemplary kindness in providing a home for the displaced of the earth, offering sanctuary to those who have been cut loose from the moorings of security and freedom in their native lands.

There are refugees in all parts of the world. When I was at the Maela refugee camp in Thailand recently, I met dedicated people who were striving daily to make the lives of the inmates as free from hardship as possible. They spoke of their concern over 'donor fatigue,' which could also translate as 'compassion fatigue.' 'Donor fatigue' expresses itself precisely in the reduction of funding. 'Compassion fatigue' expresses itself less obviously in the reduction of concern. One is the consequence of the other. Can we afford to indulge in compassion fatigue? Is the cost of meeting the needs of refugees greater than the cost that would be consequent on turning an indifferent, if not a blind, eye on their suffering? I appeal to donors the world over to fulfill the needs of these people who are in search, often it must seem to them a vain search, of refuge.

At Maela, I had valuable discussions with Thai officials responsible for the administration of Tak province where this and several other camps are situated. They acquainted me with some of the more serious problems related to refugee camps: violation of forestry laws, illegal drug use, home-brewed spirits, the problems of controlling malaria, tuberculosis, dengue fever and cholera. The concerns of the administration are as legitimate as the concerns of the refugees. Host countries also deserve consideration and practical help in coping with the difficulties related to their responsibilities.

The Ultimate Goal of Peace

Ultimately our aim should be to create a world free from the displaced, the homeless and the hopeless, a world in which each and every corner is a true sanctuary where the inhabitants will have the freedom and the capacity to live in peace. Every thought, every word, and every action that adds to the positive and the wholesome is a contribution to peace. Each and every one of us is capable of making such a contribution. Let us join hands to try to create a peaceful world where we can sleep in security and wake in happiness.

The Nobel Committee concluded its statement of 14 October 1991 with the words: "In awarding the Nobel Peace Prize ... to Aung San Suu Kyi, the Norwegian Nobel Committee wishes to honour this woman for her unflagging efforts and to show its support for the many people throughout the world who are striving to attain democracy, human rights and ethnic conciliation by peaceful means." When I joined the democracy movement in Burma, it never occurred to me that I might ever be the recipient of any prize or honour. The prize we were working for was a free, secure and just society where our people might be able to realize their full potential. The honour lay in our endeavour. History had given us the opportunity to give of our best for a cause in which we believed. When the Nobel Committee chose to honour me, the road I had chosen of my own free will became a less lonely path to follow. For this I thank the Committee, the people of Norway and peoples all over the world whose support has strengthened my faith in the common quest for peace. Thank you.

VIEWPOINT 3

> "The cold truth is that world peace, as
> it is understood through today's popu-
> list lens, would be both patently im-
> moral and manifestly dangerous."

Why "World Peace" Is Immoral and Dangerous

Miles Taylor

Miles Taylor is a political commentator and the cofounder of Partisans.org. In the following viewpoint, he maintains that world peace is a simplistic maxim that does not take into account the reality of today's geopolitical challenges. Taylor points out that the world is beset by conflicts, oppression, and slaughter, and that it may be necessary for other countries to intervene to stop horrible injustices and, in some cases, genocide. To act as isolationists and rely on the concept of world peace as the foundation of US foreign policy is immoral and dangerous. Taylor argues that until real democratic reforms take hold across the globe and liberty is universal, conflict and warfare will remain a staple.

This is an opinion piece that appeared at the Daily Caller. The views expressed do not represent the views of the Daily Caller.

As you read, consider the following questions:

1. According to Taylor, which US president once declared that wars are "as a rule to be avoided [but] they are far better than certain kinds of peace"?

2. What does the author describe as the situation in Mauritania?

3. What notorious world leader did Britain sign a peace deal with in 1938, an agreement that is now considered appeasement by the author?

Calls for intervention in Syria are becoming more urgent, and the drumbeat for air strikes against Iranian nuclear facilities is growing louder. Predictably, antiwar activists have frantically taken to the airwaves and print media to explain why [insert potential conflict here] is bad for America and for the world.

Don't worry. This is not another call for action. Rather, it is an indictment of those who reflexively urge *inaction*, no matter what the case. The Noam Chomskys of the world are busy as ever peddling the threadbare premise that wars are worse than the injustices that impel them to be launched in the first place and, therefore, we should know better than to ever use force. Doing so would be contrary to the goal of world peace!

However, everyday Americans would be wise to give more scrutiny to the seemingly redundant question, "Is world peace a good thing?"

The customary answer is nothing short of gospel to every third grader and Miss America contestant. But this overly simplistic maxim that we teach children and preach at beauty pageants is a terrible foundation for American foreign policy, at least in the way it is framed today.

41

Make no mistake. War is a grave undertaking and should in every instance be reserved—painstakingly, deliberately, stubbornly—as a last resort.

However, as Teddy Roosevelt once declared, wars are "as a rule to be avoided [but] they are far better than certain kinds of peace."

In other words, a "peace" in which some states are allowed to perpetuate abhorrent, mass crimes with impunity is not a very good peace at all.

Let's play devil's advocate for a moment, though, and assume that peace for peace's sake is desirable.

In today's world, if states were somehow prohibited from ever again engaging in hostilities with one another, would we achieve that ever elusive goal of global harmony? You tell me.

What do you call the slaughter of thousands of civilians in the streets of Syria by a despotic regime—is that "world peace"?

What do you call it when soldiers go home by home, systematically raping and killing women and children in the villages of Sudan—is that "world peace"?

Or how about the hundreds of thousands of Mauritanians who, in the twenty-first century, are forced into slavery by their own countrymen—is that "world peace"?

To the peaceniks, it is, as long as no one intervenes to stop these injustices from happening.

World leaders have often invoked this perverse paradigm of "peace" to justify simple appeasement, a statesman's cowardly antidote to the burdens of taking action. That's what happened in 1938, when British prime minister Neville Chamberlain inked a peace deal with [Adolf] Hitler and, upon returning from Berlin, declared that the agreement would bring "peace in our time."

The cold truth is that world peace, as it is understood through today's populist lens, would be both patently immoral and manifestly dangerous. We are still witness to crimes that so "shock the conscience" of mankind that they rightly justify military intervention if left unresolvable by other means.

This is not to say that real and permanent peace is impossible. That would be too bleak an assessment. But state-to-state conflict will only become obsolete when governments in all corners of the globe are controlled by their people and individual liberty is universal.

Indeed, one of the great phenomena of international relations is that no two democracies have ever gone to war with one another. A wholly democratic world is, thus, the last best hope for abolishing warfare.

Until that distant future, however, wholesale antiwar activists should be made plainly aware of the consequences of appeasement wherever they prescribe it.

Whether we intervene in Syria or assist Israel in striking Iranian nuclear facilities remains to be seen. Those should be very solemn considerations.

But one fact is clear: Ending conflict everywhere and for all time would allow injustice to persist anywhere and all the time.

> "It is time for the international security community to think seriously about preparing for a durable world peace instead of the constant threat of world war."

World Peace Needs to Be a Top Priority in International Security Circles

Scott Moore

Scott Moore is a research fellow at the Belfer Center for Science and International Affairs at Harvard University. In the following viewpoint, he suggests that as compelling evidence emerges that traditional warfare is decreasing, the international security community should be addressing the threats of ethnic and religious violence. He argues that there needs to be some serious development of institutional capabilities to deal with ethno-religious security threats instead of clinging to the old paradigm of interstate conflict. Moore says the international security community must work on three main areas of reform: prioritizing and addressing systemic socioeconomic issues, particularly income in-

equality; rethinking how militaries, diplomatic bureaucracies, and development organizations organize emergency operations and long-term institution building; and reforming the United Nations Security Council to include parties other than nation-states.

As you read, consider the following questions:

1. According to Moore, what period of modern history illustrates the threat of peace to an international security community?
2. What tiny mountain country does the author identify as the location of unimaginable ethnic slaughter in the 1990s?
3. What international security organization does the author say should broaden its participatory structures?

The very phrase "world peace" has become something of a synonym for naïveté. Yet in recent years, compelling evidence has emerged to suggest that at least one important aspect of world peace, the absence or rarity of war between countries, may in fact be close to a reality.

Scholarly work on what might be called the "decline-in-violence" phenomenon emerged following the conclusion of a surprisingly peaceful Cold War, but it has lately drawn greater popular and scholarly attention.

In a world replete with dangers, the decline-in-violence proposition is often treated with skepticism. But it is time for the international security community to think seriously about preparing for a durable world peace instead of the constant threat of world war.

To be clear, we cannot expect a violence-free world any time soon. Instead, the data suggest that certain kinds of violence, most notably interstate warfare such as the two world wars, are becoming less common even as other forms of conflict increase.

The Future of International Security

Of course, it's difficult to categorize and count acts of violence across countries. But it is a striking and little-appreciated fact that despite no shortage of violence of other kinds, the world is at present entirely and blessedly free of traditional, state-on-state warfare.

Ongoing discussions about the future of international security must include the remarkably low prevalence of interstate warfare in recent history. To be sure, the international community has made great progress in broadening the focus of security beyond conflict between countries.

But the fact remains that the basic architecture of international security is ill-equipped to function in a world in which interstate warfare is rare.

Although such wars may still occur in the future, they will be of less importance to international security than during any previous period. It is often said that soldiers prepare to fight the last war instead of the next, but the international security community has an even bigger problem: preparing for war when the future is more likely to be peace.

The Cold War

The threat of peace to an international security community fixated on war is illustrated in the history of the Cold War period and its aftermath. During this period, Western leaders erected national security structures designed to confront the threat of a theater war in Europe within the context of a global struggle for influence. Subsequently, many hundreds of thousands of lives were lost in proxy battles and interstate wars, but not in Europe.

There something quite unexpected happened: nothing. Despite millions of troops facing one another across the Iron Curtain [a term referring to the Communist bloc], a Third

Rwanda Genocide

In the first decade of the twenty-first century, the tiny central African nation of Rwanda was still recovering from the effects of a massive genocide, which can be roughly defined as the mass killing of a large group of people with the intent to destroy an ethnic, racial, national, or religious group. Over a period of one hundred days in April and May of 1994, ethnic Hutu people of Rwanda slaughtered between eight hundred thousand and one million ethnic Tutsis, as well as tens of thousands of sympathetic Hutus. In all, between 35 and 40 percent of the Rwandan population was killed or fled the violence by summer.

"Rwanda Genocide,"
Global Issues in Context Online Collection.
Detroit, MI: Gale, 2014.

World War was averted, and Western leaders turned to reaping a "peace dividend" by scaling back their far-flung entanglements.

New Threats

But these efforts were upended when the rest of the world exploded in new forms of violence for which the disarming powers were distinctly unprepared.

The Balkans were consumed in vicious internecine warfare, and the tiny mountain country of Rwanda became the scene of unimaginable ethnic slaughter in which Western countries, haunted by the specter of a failed mission in Somalia, dared not intervene.

The international community possessed neither the analytic tools nor the institutional capabilities to deal with a world order in which ethno-religious groups, and not nation-states, were the primary operative actors. Which brings us back to the question: What if organized state violence and warfare is the exception rather than the rule in international security?

The short answer is that the international community remains unprepared. Despite a decade in which the United States and many of its allies have been focused on counterinsurgency campaigns, and the US Army boasts that its junior officers routinely run municipal governments, the foreign and security policy apparatus of the great powers remain overwhelmingly focused on state-state conflict.

Washington's rapid strategic repositioning toward the Asia-Pacific region and the promulgation of an "Air-Sea Battle" doctrine is perhaps the most vivid example of an enduringly myopic focus on traditional geopolitics and the prospect of interstate warfare.

But the real risk of this approach is that it marginalizes the type of long-term capacity building which relies much more on civilian and nongovernmental actors than militaries and foreign ministries—and which is necessary in a world where unorganized, intrastate violence like that which occurred in Rwanda is the dominant issue in international security.

Doing so requires reform on at least three basic principles.

Key Reform Recommendations

First, systemic socioeconomic issues, particularly income inequality, access to basic infrastructure and services, and political participation, should become the central concerns of international security, with a correspondingly greater engagement of disciplines like sociology, anthropology, and geography.

Second, the traditional functional barriers between militaries, diplomatic bureaucracies, and development organizations should be broken down and reorganized to focus more on different time scales, with some focused on short-term emergency operations like disaster relief and humanitarian intervention, and others completely devoted to long-term, cooperative institution building.

Third, the UN [United Nations] Security Council, which traditionally represents nation-state actors, should broaden its participatory structures.

Violence is not dead, but certain forms of it, particularly interstate conflict, are in long-term decline, and that remarkable fact should be a much greater part of discussions about the future of international security.

Scholars and practitioners should engage in serious discussion about the decline of interstate warfare as a critical issue for the future of the international security community—and how it can prepare for such a happy though tentative prospect.

> "Analysing the stats reveals that, over
> the course of its history, humankind
> has seen six major declines of violence,
> including in the late 20th and early
> 21st centuries."

The World Has Never Been More Peaceful

Steven Pinker

*Steven Pinker is a linguist, experimental psychologist, scientist,
and author. In the following viewpoint, he observes that violence
in human society has decreased over time. Pinker traces this
decline-in-violence phenomenon, outlining six major trends in
world history that have enabled the decrease. He identifies the
development of nation-states to be the major factor in the decline of violence throughout history, stating that there is compelling evidence that governments are directly responsible for pacifying populations. Other pacifying forces include commerce,
cosmopolitanism, and technological advances. He argues that ac-
knowledging this profound drop in violence and the factors that
led to it are vital to continuing the trend well into the twenty-
first century.*

Steven Pinker, "Nothing to Kill or Die For," *Cosmos*, August 8, 2013. Copyright © 2013 by Cosmos. All rights reserved. Reproduced by permission.

As you read, consider the following questions:

1. According to Pinker, when was the second decline of violence on a global scale?

2. What is the percentage of deaths caused by political violence in the world since the end of the Cold War, according to the viewpoint?

3. What does Pinker identify as the biggest contributor toward global violence?

The idea that violence in human society has decreased over time invites scepticism, incredulity and sometimes anger. It hasn't been a smooth decline—and it isn't guaranteed to continue—but it is a persistent historical development, visible on scales from millennia to years, from the waging of wars to the spanking of children.

The human mind predisposes us to believe that we live in violent times—especially when stoked by news media that follows the watchwords "If it bleeds, it leads." We tend to estimate the probability of an event based on the ease with which we can recall examples, and scenes of carnage are more likely to be beamed into our homes and burned into our memories than footage of people dying of old age.

No matter how small the percentage of violent deaths may be, in absolute numbers there will always be enough to fill the evening news. This disconnects our impressions of violence from actual proportions. Also, distorting our sense of danger is part of our moral psychology: No one has ever recruited activists to a cause by announcing that the world's becoming a better place.

Nonetheless, analysing the stats reveals that, over the course of its history, humankind has seen six major declines of violence, including in the late 20th and early 21st centuries.

The First Decline

The first decline in violence happened during the transition from the anarchy of hunter-gatherer societies—which prevailed throughout most of our species' history—to the first agricultural civilisations with cities and governments, which began to emerge around 5,000 years ago.

For centuries, social theorists, such as 17th-century British philosopher Thomas Hobbes or 18th-century Swiss philosopher Jean-Jacques Rousseau, speculated from their armchairs about what life was like when humanity existed in a "state of nature". Today, we can do better. Forensic archaeology—a kind of CSI: Paleolithic—can estimate rates of violence from the proportion of skeletons in ancient sites bearing signs of trauma, such as bashed-in skulls, decapitations or arrowheads embedded in bones. Ethnographers have also tallied the causes of death in tribal peoples who in recent times lived in non-governed societies—outside the control of a centralised state.

These investigations show that, on average, around 15% of 'non-state' people met their ends through violence, compared with about 3% of citizens of the earliest states. Three per cent, by the way, is also the most pessimistic estimate of the rate of death in the 20th century from all wars, genocides and human-caused famines combined.

Tribal violence commonly subsides when a state or empire imposes control over a territory and its people, leading to the various 'Paxes' that are familiar to readers of history (for example, the 207-year Pax Romana from 27 BC to 180 AD). It's not that these kings and emperors had a benevolent interest in their citizens' welfare. Subjects who raid and feud just shuffle resources or settle scores among themselves, but from the ruler's point of view this represents a dead loss: foregone opportunities to extract taxes, tributes, soldiers, serfs and slaves.

The Second Decline

After this first major transition, the second decline of violence is best documented in Europe, where in many places homicide records go back centuries. Narrative histories of the Middle Ages highlight the brutality of everyday life. As U.S. author and historian Barbara Tuchman put it, medieval knights fought "with furious gusto and a single strategy, which consisted in trying to ruin the enemy by killing and maiming as many of his peasants . . . as possible."

Highwaymen made travel outside cities a risk to life and limb. Dinners were commonly enlivened by dagger attacks. So many people had their noses cut off that medieval medical textbooks speculated about techniques for growing them back.

From the late Middle Ages to the 20th century, European countries experienced a 10- to 50-fold decline in homicide rates. Historians attribute this to the consolidation of a patchwork of feudal territories into large kingdoms with centralised authority and an infrastructure of commerce. Criminal justice was nationalised, and zero-sum plunder gave way to positive-sum trade. These developments encouraged a 'civilising process', in which people increasingly controlled their impulses and sought to cooperate with their neighbours.

The Third Decline

The third transition—sometimes called the Humanitarian Revolution—took off around the Enlightenment in the 18th century. Governments and churches had long maintained order by punishing nonconformists with mutilation, torture and gruesome forms of execution, such as burning at the stake, breaking on the wheel, disembowelment, impalement through the rectum, and hanging a person by the ankles and sawing him or her in half from the crotch down. The 18th century saw a cascade of abolitions of judicial torture, including the prohibition of "cruel and unusual punishment" in the Eighth Amendment to the U.S. Constitution.

At the same time, countries began to whittle down their list of capital crimes from the hundreds (including poaching, sodomy, witchcraft, concealing birth and counterfeiting) to murder and treason. A growing wave of countries abolished blood sports, duelling, witch hunts, religious persecution, despotism and slavery.

The Fourth Decline

Fast-forward to the modern era, where the fourth major decline in violence is seen directly after the end of World War II. The second half of the 20th century witnessed a historically unprecedented development: The world's great powers, and developed states in general, stopped waging war on one another. Today, we take it for granted that France and Germany or Britain and Russia won't come to blows. But centuries ago, the great powers were almost always at war, and until recently, Western European countries initiated two to three wars every year. Historians sometimes refer to this recent respite from major interstate war as the Long Peace.

The Fifth Decline

The fifth trend involves war in the rest of the world. Since 1946, several organisations have meticulously tracked armed conflicts and their human toll worldwide. For several decades, a bulge of civil wars accompanied the decline of interstate wars, as newly independent countries in the developing world were led by inept governments, challenged by insurgencies, and armed by Cold War superpowers.

The Sixth Decline

But civil wars tend to kill far fewer people than wars between states. And since the end of the Cold War in 1989, organised conflicts of all kinds—civil wars, genocides, repression by autocratic governments and terrorist attacks—have waned throughout the world, and their death tolls have dropped even more precipitously. The rate of documented direct deaths from political violence (war, terrorism, genocide and warlord militias) in the past decade, when compared to overall deaths in the world population, is just a few hundredths of a percentage point. Even if we multiplied the rate to account for unrecorded deaths and the victims of war-caused disease and famine, it still wouldn't come close to 1%.

The post-war era has seen a growing revulsion against aggression on smaller scales, including violence against ethnic minorities, women, children, homosexuals and animals. These spin-offs from the concept of human rights have been asserted in a cascade of rights revolutions. . . .

Reasons for Decline

Why has violence declined on so many scales of time and magnitude?

Is it because violence has been bred out of us, leaving us more peaceful by nature? This seems unlikely. Natural selection has a speed limit measured in generations, and many of the declines have unfolded over decades or even years. Toddlers kick, bite and hit; little boys play-fight; people of all ages continue to snipe and bicker, and most of them continue to harbour violent fantasies and enjoy violent entertainment.

It's more likely that human nature has always comprised inclinations toward violence and inclinations that counteract them—what Abraham Lincoln called "the better angels of our nature"—and that historical circumstances have increasingly favoured our better angels.

Violent Tendencies

So what parts of human nature militate toward violence? I count five, depending on how you lump or split them. There's raw exploitation—seeking something that you want where a living being happens to be in the way; examples include rape, plunder, conquest and the elimination of rivals. There's nothing particularly fancy in the psychology of this kind of violence other than a zeroing out of whatever inclinations generally inhibit us from that kind of exploitation.

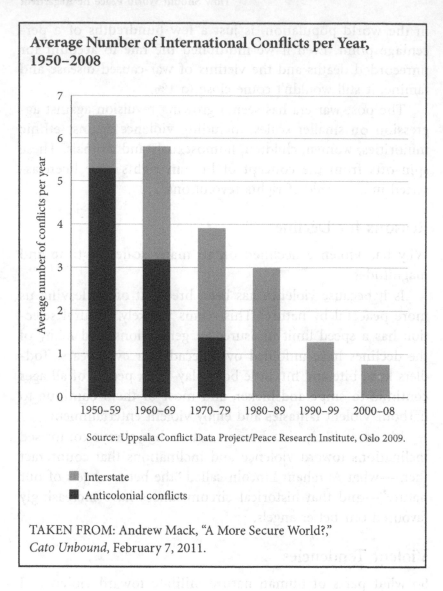

Average Number of International Conflicts per Year, 1950–2008

Average number of conflicts per year

Source: Uppsala Conflict Data Project/Peace Research Institute, Oslo 2009.

■ Interstate
■ Anticolonial conflicts

TAKEN FROM: Andrew Mack, "A More Secure World?," *Cato Unbound*, February 7, 2011.

Other violent tendencies include the drive toward dominance; both competition among individuals to be the alpha male, and competition among groups for ethnic, racial, national or religious supremacy or preeminence. Then there's the thirst for revenge, the kind of moralistic violence that inspires vendettas, 'rough justice' and cruel punishments.

The biggest contributor of all is ideology: militant religions, nationalism, fascism, Nazism and communism, which lead to large-scale violence via a pernicious cost-benefit analysis. What these ideologies have in common is that they posit a utopia that is infinitely good for infinitely long. You do the math: If the ends are infinitely good, then the means can be arbitrarily violent and you're still on the positive side of the moral ledger.

How Are Violent Tendencies Controlled?

The better angels that mitigate these inclinations include the faculties of self-control, empathy, moral sense and fairness. Moral sense goes in both directions: It can push people to be more or less violent, depending on how it is deployed. Then there is reason; the cognitive faculties that allow us to engage in objective, detached analysis.

The crucial question is: Which historical developments bring out our better angels? The most obvious is the concept of the Leviathan—an idea introduced by Hobbes that describes a state with a monopoly on the legitimate use of force. A disinterested judiciary and police force can defuse the temptation of exploitative attack, inhibit the impulse for revenge, and circumvent the self-serving biases that make all parties believe they are on the side of good.

We saw evidence for the pacifying effects of government in the way that the rates of killing went down after the expansion and consolidation of states in tribal societies and in medieval Europe. And we can watch the movie in reverse when violence erupts in zones of anarchy such as the Wild West, in failed states or in neighbourhoods controlled by mafias and street gangs, who can't call on the state to defend their interests, but have to administer their own rough justice.

The Role of Commerce

Another pacifying force is commerce, a game in which everybody can win. As technological progress enables the exchange of goods and ideas over longer distances and among larger groups of trading partners, other people become more valuable alive than dead, and they switch from being targets of demonisation and dehumanisation to being partners in reciprocal altruism. Though the relationship between the U.S. and China is far from warm, the U.S. is unlikely to declare war on China or vice versa: They make too much of the stuff the U.S. consumes; the U.S. owes them too much money. Several studies show that countries with open economies participate in fewer state wars and have fewer civil wars and genocides, holding all else constant.

Another peacemaker is cosmopolitanism, the expansion of people's parochial little worlds through literacy, mobility, education, science, history, journalism and mass media. These forms of virtual reality can prompt people to appreciate the perspective of people unlike themselves and expand their circle of sympathy to embrace them.

The same technologies have powered an expansion of rationality and objectivity in human affairs. It is probably no coincidence that the Humanitarian Revolution came on the heels of the Age of Reason and the Enlightenment, that the Long Peace and Rights Revolutions coincided with the electronic global village, and that the recent Arab Spring blossomed in the age of the Internet and social media.

Whatever its causes, the implications of the historical decline of violence could not be more profound. What could be more fundamental to our sense of meaning and purpose than a conception of whether the strivings of the human race over long stretches of time have left us better or worse off?

How, in particular, are we to make sense of modernity—the erosion of family, tribe, tradition and religion by the forces of individualism, cosmopolitanism, reason and science? So much depends on how we understand the legacy of this transition: whether we see our world as a nightmare of crime, terrorism, genocide and war, or as a period that, in the light of the historical and statistical facts, is blessed by unprecedented levels of peaceful coexistence.

Perhaps most importantly, the decline of violence emboldens us to try to isolate, concentrate and bottle the special ingredients that have made it possible. A better understanding of what drove the numbers down can steer us toward doing things that make people better off, rather than just congratulating ourselves on how moral we are.

| "*History shows that wars often start because of miscalculation.*"

World Peace Requires Pragmatism and Clear Vision

Kim R. Holmes

Kim R. Holmes is a distinguished fellow at the Heritage Foundation. In the following viewpoint, he criticizes the national security strategy of the Barack Obama administration, charging that the president and his national security team have let wishful thinking trump reality when it comes to assessing geopolitical threats. One disturbing example is the administration's conventional wisdom on Russia: Russia's recent aggressive actions in Crimea and Ukraine signal that Russia can be a real threat. Holmes points to China as another example of the Obama administration's miscalculations when it comes to security threats to the United States. He concludes that it is imperative for President Obama to adjust his strategic thinking on these matters, acknowledge that US military strength is essential to deter these growing threats, and realize the way to peace is a strong and pragmatic security policy.

As you read, consider the following questions:

1. According to Holmes, what country did Russia invade in 2014?

2. What did Princeton University professor Aaron L. Friedberg say about the US relationship with China?

3. To what other US president does Holmes compare President Obama?

"To succeed, we must face the world as it is."

So the [Barack Obama] administration declared in its 2010 National Security Strategy statement.

That should be a truism in national security strategy. Unfortunately, the administration has let wishful thinking trump reality.

Its conventional wisdom has been that rivalries between great powers were things of the past. The balance of power didn't matter anymore. Russia was too weak and preoccupied to be a real threat. China's hunger for economic development and international trade would restrain its military ambitions. Large militaries were, therefore, passé. All that's needed are drones and other high-tech weaponry to fight low-intensity conflicts. When backed with sufficient goodwill for "international cooperation," that's all it takes to establish a new kind of order.

It may be time to revisit this bit of conventional wisdom.

A Reassessment of U.S. Security Challenges

Moscow has invaded Crimea and may take further military action in Ukraine. While it is true that Russian power is a shadow of its former Soviet self, it is not true that it is some military lightweight in its own region. Russia sees itself as America's rival, but it's not the old global competition among ideologies or between huge standing armies, but a regional rivalry over influence, access and values in Russia's "near abroad" and the Middle East (and even inside Russia itself). The president may not see Ukraine as "some Cold War chessboard in which we're in competition with Russia," but [Russian president] Vladimir Putin surely does, which is why he's acting more decisively than the obviously confused Barack Obama.

Which raises the question: If Russia sees itself as our rival, and we don't, whose rules are we playing by? Theirs or ours?

The same question may be asked of China. A few years ago, it was considered impolite to talk about China's rising power as a threat. Today, many experts agree with Princeton University professor Aaron L. Friedberg that, "Over the course of the next several decades, there is a good chance that the United States will find itself engaged in an open and intense geopolitical rivalry with the People's Republic of China."

If the administration wants to believe that China will never jeopardize economic development with military ambitions, it has some explaining to do. Does desire for trade, wealth and energy really account for China's aggressive pursuit of its territorial and maritime ambitions? Surely if there ever was a conflict that could derail China's economic development, it would be some fruitless war over a tiny uninhabited island in the East China Sea.

China's obsession with ever-expanding "core" interests and its desire to establish a "new type of major power relations" sounds like great power politics to me. It appears to want to divvy up interests with the United States the way Prussia, Austria and Russia once did in Poland in the age of great power rivalries in Europe. This worldview may not be our cup of tea, but it is surely theirs.

Foreign Policy Myopia

Why does it matter that we are playing by different rules? We are in the midst of one of the biggest military drawdowns in

Vladimir Putin

Vladimir Putin is a Russian politician who has served as president of Russia since 2012. Formerly an agent of the Soviet intelligence agency the KGB during the Cold War era, he lived undercover for a decade and a half. Putin then suddenly entered politics in the early 1990s and subsequently saw a meteoric rise. By August of 1999, ailing president Boris Yeltsin appointed him prime minister, and when Yeltsin stepped down that December, Putin became the acting president. Many were wary of his background in the KGB, which had a reputation for human rights abuses, and were also concerned about his status as a relative newcomer to politics. However, he won the popular election in March of 2000 to retain his post as president. Although his popularity was such that he easily won a second term in 2004, his approval rating soon began to plummet. He served as president until 2008 and then as prime minister until 2012. In 2012 Putin was again elected president of Russia. He came to international attention again in 2014 when he invaded the Ukrainian peninsula of Crimea and annexed it to Russia in what became known as the Crimean crisis.

"Vladimir Putin," Biography in Context.
Detroit, MI: Gale, 2014.

recent history. The hard power of the United States necessary to manage these rivalries is weakening rapidly. We've convinced ourselves that we don't need these forces anymore largely because we believe that great power rivalries are a thing of the past.

This is a delusion. History shows that wars often start because of miscalculation. This often happens when the competitors misunderstand the balance of power. We may very well be witnessing this problem playing out today in Ukraine. Like Jimmy Carter after the Soviet invasion of Afghanistan, President Obama seems shocked by Mr. Putin's invasion of Crimea, and disoriented by the realization that Mr. Putin's behavior doesn't fit his worldview. Out of such misunderstandings wars are made, precisely because the leaders are chasing fantasies instead of reality.

Correcting Mr. Obama's strategic myopia is a long-term challenge. For starters, it means accepting that, for America, the purpose of the balance of power is peace, not war. And the right goal of U.S. military strength is deterrence, not military intervention. Not facing the world as it really is actually raises the risk of war.

Periodical and Internet Sources Bibliography

The following articles have been selected to supplement the diverse views presented in this chapter.

BBC	"Is World Peace Possible?," November 12, 2012.
Tom Boyd	"Is Peace on Earth Even Possible?," *Denver Post*, December 20, 2014.
Cole Connelly and Matt Kettmann	"Paul Chappell: Making World Peace Possible," *Santa Barbara Independent* (California), December 22, 2011.
Adam Frank	"What Would You Give Up for World Peace?," NPR, August 3, 2014.
Talia Hagerty	"The World Is Getting Less Peaceful Every Year," *Pacific Standard*, July 10, 2014.
Z Pallo Jordan	"Western Interventions Undermine World Peace," *BusinessDay*, June 26, 2014.
Tony Karon	"The Year in War and Peace: World Leaders Prove Era of Visionaries Over," Al Jazeera America, December 29, 2013.
Lillie Leonardi	"Let There Be Peace," *Huffington Post*, August 5, 2014.
Michael Lind	"The World Is Actually More Peaceful than Ever," Salon.com, April 23, 2013.
CJ Werleman	"We're Living Through the 'Most Peaceful Era' in Human History—With One Big Exception," Salon.com, January 15, 2014.

OPPOSING
VIEWPOINTS®
SERIES

CHAPTER 2

How Can World Peace Be Established?

Chapter Preface

In the early morning of August 21, 2013, several rockets were fired into Ghouta, a largely agricultural area outside the city of Damascus in Syria, an Arab nation embroiled in a bloody civil war. At the time of the attack, the area was being held by Syrian rebel forces that were fighting to oust Syria's president, Bashar al-Assad. As the rockets exploded on contact, they released sarin. Classified by the United Nations as a weapon of mass destruction, sarin is a lethal chemical gas that causes muscle paralysis and leads to suffocation only minutes after inhalation. The Ghouta sarin attack resulted in the deaths of more than fourteen hundred civilians. It is widely believed that the Syrian government was behind the atrocity.

The conflict in Syria had erupted in March 2011 when protesters gathered in large numbers to demand democratic reform and the release of political prisoners, as well as to express opposition to widespread political and bureaucratic corruption and civil rights violations by the police. Assad called for a brutal crackdown on the peaceful protesters. Over the next several months, scores of protesters were beaten in the streets, imprisoned, tortured, and even killed. Opposition to the Assad regime turned into an armed rebellion. By early 2012, nearly eight thousand people had died and hundreds of thousands were displaced as a result of the conflict.

The chemical weapons attack on Ghouta resulted in widespread condemnation of the Assad regime. On the same day, the United Nations (UN) called for an emergency session of the UN Security Council. Western countries formulated a resolution to demand a full investigation of the incident, but efforts were stymied by strong opposition from Russia and China.

Frustrated by the lack of international action, the United States took the lead. On September 10, 2013, US president

Barack Obama stated that the world had a moral obligation—and a security interest—in taking action against Assad. "If we fail to act, the Assad regime will see no reason to stop using chemical weapons," he warned. "As the ban against these weapons erodes, other tyrants will have no reason to think twice about acquiring poison gas and using them."

In his remarks, Obama outlined the US response to Assad's use of chemical weapons: The United States would carry out targeted military strikes on Syrian chemical weapons targets to degrade Assad's ability to use them against the rebels and civilian populations.

As a military solution to the problem of Syria's chemical weapons was being planned, a diplomatic solution was also emerging. In early September, US secretary of state John Kerry suggested, in an offhanded way, that Syria could avoid military strikes if it turned over all of its chemical weapons in a week. That rhetorical comment by Kerry led to negotiations between the United States and Russia to eliminate Syria's stockpile of chemical weapons. Syria agreed to give up its chemical weapons by June 2014 and to abide by the Chemical Weapons Convention, an international treaty that outlaws the production, stockpile, and use of chemical weapons. On June 23, 2014, it was reported that the final stockpile of chemical weapons was shipped out of Syria to be destroyed under the supervision of the Organisation for the Prohibition of Chemical Weapons (OPCW).

The US response to Syria's use of chemical weapons generated a much larger discussion over America's role in international conflicts. That debate is included in the following chapter, which explores various ways to bring about world peace. Other viewpoints in the chapter examine the effectiveness of a strong international order, the role of democracy in establishing world peace, and the impact of regional integration as a barrier to conflict.

> *"The U.S. has so far been prepared to act as the guarantor of international stability, but may not be willing—or able—to do so indefinitely."*

A Stable and Effective International Order Can Secure World Peace

Margaret MacMillan

Margaret MacMillan is an author, historian, and professor of international history at Oxford University. In the following viewpoint, she suggests that the centennial of the start of World War I offers people a chance to reflect on the value of world peace and on how quickly misunderstandings, human error, and sudden catastrophes can blow up into major conflicts. MacMillan points out that the world is in transition: The United States may not be willing to play the role of the world's policeman for much longer, and there is no clear-cut power to succeed it. She says the best option for a durable world peace is a stable and effective international order, but nations have been slow to come together and work cooperatively for global good.

As you read, consider the following questions:

1. According to the author, how many combatants were killed during World War I?

2. How many articles, treatises, and books on World War I does the author estimate have been published in English?

3. When did the Bosnian War end, according to MacMillan?

Earlier this year [2013] I was on holiday in Corsica and happened to wander into the church of a tiny hamlet in the hills where I found a memorial to the dead from World War I. Out of a population that can have been no more than 150, eight young men, bearing among them only three last names, had died in that conflict. Such lists can be found all over Europe, in great cities and in small villages. Similar memorials are spread around the globe, for the Great War, as it was known prior to 1940, also drew soldiers from Asia, Africa, and North America.

World War I still haunts us, partly because of the sheer scale of the carnage—10 million combatants killed and many more wounded. Countless civilians lost their lives, too, whether through military action, starvation, or disease. Whole empires were destroyed and societies brutalized.

But there's another reason the war continues to haunt us: We still cannot agree why it happened. Was it caused by the overweening ambitions of some of the men in power at the time? Kaiser Wilhelm II and his ministers, for example, wanted a greater Germany with a global reach, so they challenged the naval supremacy of Great Britain. Or does the explanation lie in competing ideologies? National rivalries? Or in the sheer and seemingly unstoppable momentum of militarism? As an arms race accelerated, generals and admirals made plans that became ever more aggressive as well as rigid. Did that make an explosion inevitable?

Or would it never have happened had a random event in an Austro-Hungarian backwater not lit the fuse? In the second year of the conflagration that engulfed most of Europe, a bitter joke made the rounds: "Have you seen today's headline? 'Archduke Found Alive: War a Mistake.'" That is the most dispiriting explanation of all—that the war was simply a blunder that could have been avoided.

The search for explanations began almost as soon as the guns opened fire in the summer of 1914 and has never stopped. Scholars have combed through archives from Belgrade to Berlin looking for the causes. An estimated 32,000 articles, treatises, and books on World War I have been published in English alone. So when a British publisher took me out to lunch on a lovely spring day in Oxford five years ago and asked me if I would like to try my hand at one of history's greatest puzzles, my first reaction was a firm no. Yet afterward I could not stop thinking about this question that has haunted so many. In the end I succumbed. The result is yet another book, my own effort to understand what happened a century ago and why.

It was not just academic curiosity that drove me, but a sense of urgency as well. If we cannot determine how one of the most momentous conflicts in history happened, how can we hope to avoid another such catastrophe in the future?

The Lessons of World War I for Today

Just look at the actual and potential conflicts that dominate the news today. The Middle East, made up largely of countries that received their present borders as a consequence of World War I, is but one of many areas around the globe that is in turmoil, and has been for decades. Now there's a civil war in Syria, which has raised the spectre of a wider conflict in the region while also troubling relations among the major powers and testing their diplomatic skills. The Bashar al-Assad regime's use of poison gas—a weapon first deployed in the

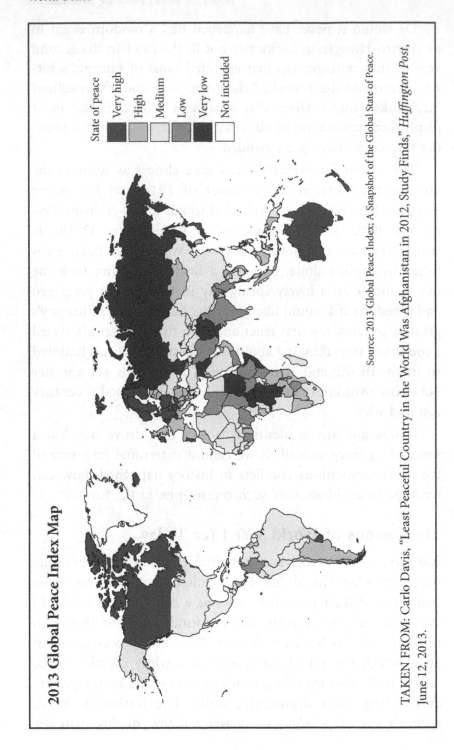

2013 Global Peace Index Map

State of peace

Very high
High
Medium
Low
Very low
Not included

Source: 2013 Global Peace Index: A Snapshot of the Global State of Peace.

TAKEN FROM: Carlo Davis, "Least Peaceful Country in the World Was Afghanistan in 2012, Study Finds," *Huffington Post*, June 12, 2013.

trench warfare of 1914, then outlawed because world opinion viewed it as barbaric—nearly precipitated American air strikes. Commentary on these developments was filled with references to the guns of that long-ago August. Just as policy makers then discovered they had started something they could not stop, so this past summer we feared that such air strikes might lead to a wider and more long-lasting conflict than anyone in President Barack Obama's administration could foresee.

The one-hundredth anniversary of 1914 should make us reflect anew on our vulnerability to human error, sudden catastrophes, and sheer accident. So we have good reason to glance over our shoulders even as we look ahead. History, said Mark Twain, never repeats itself but it rhymes. The past cannot provide us with clear blueprints for how to act, for it offers such a multitude of lessons that it leaves us free to pick and choose among them to suit our own political and ideological inclinations. Still, if we can see past our blinders and take note of the telling parallels between then and now, the ways in which our world resembles that of a hundred years ago, history does give us valuable warnings.

Wanted: A World Policeman

Britain, which once played an international leadership role during the 19th and the first part of the 20th centuries, in the end found the demands too great and the costs too high. After World War II, the British people were no longer willing and the British economy no longer capable of sustaining such a role.

The U.S. has so far been prepared to act as the guarantor of international stability, but may not be willing—or able—to do so indefinitely. Over a century ago, at a time when it was well launched on its rise to world-power status and in the process of translating its huge and growing economic strength into military and foreign policy, it began to assume the mantle of leadership. Teddy Roosevelt and Woodrow Wilson, though they were two very different types of men, shared the feeling that the U.S. had a moral obligation to the world. "We have become a great nation," Roosevelt said, "and we must behave as beseems a people with such responsibilities." Since then, there have been times when isolationist sentiments have threatened this commitment, but the U.S. has for the most part remained deeply engaged in world affairs, through World War II, to the effort to contain Soviet aggression during the Cold War, and to the present global war on terrorism. With the collapse of the Soviet Union and its empire at the end of the 1980s, the U.S., perhaps without reflecting, continued to act as the world's hegemon, assuming responsibilities that ranged from stabilizing the international economy to ensuring security. The long agony of Bosnia finally came to an end in 1995 when American pressure in combination with NATO [North Atlantic Treaty Organization] military action persuaded the Serbs to enter into the Dayton Agreement. And although America's actions in Iraq and Libya were certainly not met with universal acclaim, even in the U.S. itself, Saddam Hussein and Muammar Gaddafi had few friends and many enemies by the time they met their ends at American hands.

Today, however, the U.S., while still the strongest power in the world, is not as powerful as it once was. It has suffered military setbacks in Iraq and Afghanistan, and has had difficulty finding allies who will stand by it, as the current Syrian crisis demonstrates. Uncomfortably aware that they have few reliable friends and many potential enemies, the Americans are now considering a return to a more isolationist policy.

The Future of Peace

Is the U.S. now reaching the end of its tether, as Britain did before it? If it retreats even partially from its global role, which powers will dominate the international order, and what will that mean for the prospects of world peace?

It is difficult to guess what might come next. Russia may dream of its Soviet past when it was a superpower, but with a chaotic economy and a declining population its ambitions far outrun its capacities. China is a rising power but its preoccupations are likely to be focused on Asia. Further afield it will concentrate, as it is doing at present, on securing the resources it needs for its economy, while probably being reluctant to intervene in far-off conflicts where it has little at stake. The European Union talks of a world role but so far has shown little inclination to develop its military resources, and its internal divisions make it increasingly difficult for Brussels to get agreement on foreign policy. The countries in the BRICS group—Brazil, Russia, India, China, and South Africa—are joined together more in theory than reality. The hope of a coalition of democracies, from Asia to America, willing to intervene in the name of humanitarianism or international stability, reminds me of the old story of the mice and the cat—who is going to be first to put the bell around the animal's neck? As for public opinion, the citizenry within individual countries, preoccupied with domestic issues, has become increasingly unwilling to fund or take part in foreign adventures.

It may take a moment of real danger to force the major powers of this new world order to come together in coalitions able and willing to act. Action, if it does come, may be too little and too late, and the price we all pay for that delay may well be high. Instead of muddling along from one crisis to another, now is the time to think again about those dreadful lessons of a century ago in the hope that our leaders, with our encouragement, will think about how they can work together to build a stable international order.

| *"We are, in short, moving to a multipolar world."*

Regional Integration and Cooperation Can Establish a Lasting Peace

Jeffrey D. Sachs

Jeffrey D. Sachs is an author, a professor, the director of the Earth Institute at Columbia University, and a special advisor to the United Nations secretary-general. In the following viewpoint, he contends that regional integration is one of the few solutions to long-festering problems between neighboring countries. Sachs points out that the decline of American global power over the past several years will necessitate more regional cooperation and may result in a more stable international order. He offers the European Union as an example of this kind of institutional framework, maintaining that the integration of European nations has led to environmental, political, and economic benefits overall. Sachs argues that the formation of such regional powers in East Asia, Latin America, South Asia, and the Middle East has tremendous potential to secure peace and stability.

As you read, consider the following questions:

1. According to Sachs, which European Union (EU) countries have experienced recent economic crises?

2. In what decade did Egyptian leader Gamal Abdel Nasser launch a call for Arab unity?

3. How much money does Sachs report that the United States was able to offer to aid Egypt in 2011?

In almost every part of the world, long-festering problems can be solved through closer cooperation among neighboring countries. The European Union [EU] provides the best model for how neighbors that have long fought each other can come together for mutual benefit. Ironically, today's decline in American global power may lead to more effective regional cooperation.

The Achievements of the European Union

This may seem an odd time to praise the EU, given the economic crises in Greece, Spain, Portugal, and Ireland. Europe has not solved the problem of balancing the interests of strong economies in the north and those of weaker economies in the south. Still, the EU's accomplishments vastly outweigh its current difficulties.

The EU has created a zone of peace where once there was relentless war. It has provided the institutional framework for reuniting Western and Eastern Europe. It has fostered regional-scale infrastructure. The single market has been crucial to making Europe one of the most prosperous places on the planet. And the EU has been a global leader on environmental sustainability.

For these reasons, the EU provides a unique model for other regions that remain stuck in a mire of conflict, poverty, lack of infrastructure, and environmental crisis. New regional organizations, such as the African Union, look to the EU as a role model for regional problem solving and integration. Yet, to this day, most regional groupings remain too weak to solve their members' pressing problems.

Sowing Division

In most other regions, ongoing political divisions have their roots in the Cold War or the colonial era. During the Cold War, neighbors often competed with each other by "choosing sides"—allying themselves with either the United States or the Soviet Union. Pakistan tilted towards the Americans; India towards the Soviets. Countries had little incentive to make peace with their neighbors as long as they enjoyed the financial support of the US or the USSR [Soviet Union]. On the contrary, continued conflict often led directly to more financial aid.

Indeed, the US and Europe often acted to undermine regional integration, which they believed would limit their roles as power brokers. Thus, when [Egyptian leader] Gamal Abdel Nasser launched a call for Arab unity in the 1950s, the US and Europe viewed him as a threat. The US undercut his call for strong Arab cooperation and nationalism, fearing a loss of American influence in the Middle East. As a result, Nasser increasingly aligned Egypt with the Soviet Union, and ultimately failed in the quest to unite Arab interests.

A New World Order

Today's reality, however, is that great powers can no longer divide and conquer other regions, even if they try. The age of colonialism is finished, and we are now moving beyond the age of US global dominance.

Recent events in the Middle East and Central Asia, for example, clearly reflect the decline of US influence. America's failure to win any lasting geopolitical advantage through the use of military force in Iraq and Afghanistan underscore the limits of its power, while its budget crisis ensures that it will cut its military resources sooner rather than later. Similarly,

© Betsy Streeter/Cartoonstock.com.

the US played no role in the political revolutions under way in the Arab world, and still has not demonstrated any clear policy response to them.

President Barack Obama's recent speech [in May 2011] on the Middle East is a further display of America's declining influence in the region. The speech drew the most attention for calling on Israel to return to its 1967 borders, but the effect was undercut when Israel flatly rejected the US position. The world could see that there would be little practical follow-up.

The rest of the speech was even more revealing, though it drew little public notice. When Obama discussed the Arab political upheavals, he noted the importance of economic development. Yet when it came to US action, the most that the US could offer financially was slight debt relief for Egypt ($1 billion), scant loan guarantees ($1 billion), and some insurance coverage for private investments.

The real message was that the US government would contribute very little financially to the region's economic recovery. The days when a country could depend on large-scale American financing are over.

The Rise of Regional Cooperation

We are, in short, moving to a multipolar world. The Cold War's end has not led to greater US dominance, but rather to the dissemination of global power to many regions. East Asia, South Asia, Latin America, and the Middle East have new geopolitical and economic influence. Each region, increasingly, must find its own path to economic development, energy and food security, and effective infrastructure, and must do so in a world threatened by climate change and resource scarcity.

Each region, therefore, will have to secure its own future. Of course, this should occur in a context of cooperation across regions as well as within them.

The Middle East is in a strong position to help itself. There is a high degree of economic complementarity between Egypt and the oil-rich Gulf states. Egypt can supply technology, manpower, and considerable expertise for the Arab region, while the Gulf provides energy and finance, as well as some specialists. The long-delayed vision of Arab economic unity should be returned to the table.

Israel, too, should recognize that its long-term security and prosperity will be enhanced as part of an economically stronger region. For the sake of its own national interests, Israel must come to terms with its neighbors.

Other regions also will find that the decline of US power increases the urgency of stronger cooperation between neighbors. Some of the greatest tensions in the world—say India and Pakistan, or North and South Korea—should be defused as part of region-wide strengthening. As the EU shows, ancient enmities and battle lines can be turned into mutually beneficial cooperation if a region looks forward, to resolving its long-term needs, rather than backward, to its long-standing rivalries and conflicts.

| "One of the few truly robust findings in international relations is that established democracies never go to war with one another."

Democracy Leads to Peace and Greater Prosperity

Mark P. Lagon

Mark P. Lagon is an author and adjunct senior fellow for human rights at the Council on Foreign Relations. In the following viewpoint, he suggests that supporting the spread of democracy holds tangible benefits for both the United States and the world. Democratic countries tend to be more peaceful because both domestic and foreign policies usually flow from consensus and moderation; democracy enhances economic development, which leads to more prosperity; and democracy offers more opportunities and civil rights to women, migrants, and religious and ethnic minorities. Lagon underscores that the effort to facilitate democratic reform around the world should be a result of multilateral action and transparent means to ensure legitimacy. One effective way to do this is through the support of civic organizations.

As you read, consider the following questions:

1. According to Lagon, what country had a significant role in widening democracy in Western Europe after World War II?

2. What US president does Lagon identify as the one who elevated democratization in the Middle East as a strategic priority after the terrorist attacks of September 11, 2001?

3. In what year did United Nations secretary-general Kofi A. Annan launch the UN Democracy Fund (UNDEF) to fund a range of civil society organizations?

Furthering democracy is often dismissed as moralism distinct from U.S. interests or mere lip service to build support for strategic policies. Yet there are tangible stakes for the United States and indeed the world in the spread of democracy—namely, greater peace, prosperity, and pluralism. Controversial means for promoting democracy and frequent mismatches between deeds and words have clouded appreciation of this truth.

Democracies often have conflicting priorities, and democracy promotion is not a panacea. Yet one of the few truly robust findings in international relations is that established democracies never go to war with one another. Foreign policy "realists" advocate working with other governments on the basis of interests, irrespective of character, and suggest that this approach best preserves stability in the world. However, durable stability flows from a domestic politics built on consensus and peaceful competition, which more often than not promotes similar international conduct for governments.

There has long been controversy about whether democracy enhances economic development. The dramatic growth of China certainly challenges this notion. Still, history will likely show that democracy yields the most prosperity. Notwithstanding the global financial turbulence of the past three years, democracy's elements facilitate long-term economic growth. These elements include above all freedom of expression and learning to promote innovation, and rule of law to foster predictability for investors and stop corruption from stunting growth. It is for that reason that the UN [United Nations] Development Programme (UNDP) and the 2002 UN Financing for Development conference in Monterrey, Mexico, embraced good governance as the enabler of development. These elements have unleashed new emerging powers such as India and Brazil and raised the quality of life for impoverished peoples. Those who argue that economic development will eventually yield political freedoms may be reversing the order of influences—or at least discounting the reciprocal relationship between political and economic liberalization.

Finally, democracy affords all groups equal access to justice—and equal opportunity to shine as assets in a country's economy. Democracy's support for pluralism prevents human assets—including religious and ethnic minorities, women, and migrants—from being squandered. Indeed, a shortage of economic opportunities and outlets for grievances has contributed significantly to the ongoing upheaval in the Middle East. Pluralism is also precisely what is needed to stop violent extremism from wreaking havoc on the world.

Evolving U.S. Policy

To say there are major interests in democracy's "enlargement"—that central concept in both national security strategy blueprints of the [Bill] Clinton presidency—does not settle what role the United States should play and what policy tools are appropriate. These are the questions not of why but of how. A look at waves of U.S. policy since World War II offers apt lessons.

After World War II, the United States played a significant role in deepening and widening democracy in Western Eu-

Democracy and American Foreign Policy

Democracy and respect for human rights have long been central components of U.S. foreign policy. Supporting democracy not only promotes such fundamental American values as religious freedom and worker rights, but also helps create a more secure, stable, and prosperous global arena in which the United States can advance its national interests. In addition, democracy is the one national interest that helps to secure all the others. Democratically governed nations are more likely to secure the peace, deter aggression, expand open markets, promote economic development, protect American citizens, combat international terrorism and crime, uphold human and worker rights, avoid humanitarian crises and refugee flows, improve the global environment, and protect human health.

With these goals in mind, the United States seeks to:

- Promote democracy as a means to achieve security, stability, and prosperity for the entire world;
- Assist newly formed democracies in implementing democratic principles;
- Assist democracy advocates around the world to establish vibrant democracies in their own countries; and
- Identify and denounce regimes that deny their citizens the right to choose their leaders in elections that are free, fair, and transparent.

"Democracy," US Department of State, 2014.

rope. The United States encouraged European integration to stabilize the West European democracies, and NATO [North

Atlantic Treaty Organization] was a bulwark within which Italy, West Germany, Portugal, and Spain democratized. Later, after the Cold War, the twin institutions of NATO and an integrated Europe together created powerful incentives for emerging East European democracies to join Western multilateral institutions.

Cold War competition with the Soviet Union, however, frequently led the United States to support illiberal governments. (President Franklin D. Roosevelt's revealing quip about Nicaraguan dictator Anastasio Somoza—"He may be a bastard, but he's our bastard"—too often became U.S. policy during the Cold War years.) Eventually, a consensus emerged in the 1980s—arguably President Ronald Reagan's greatest legacy—that the United States had strategic interests in urging its autocratic Latin American and East Asian allies toward democracy. And so, in the 1980s, the United States supported land reforms in El Salvador that were deeply unpopular among ruling elites; facilitated the departure of General Augusto Pinochet as Chile's leader; and pushed Taiwan, South Korea, and the Philippines in the direction of veritable electoral democracy.

After 9/11 [referring to the September 11, 2001, terrorist attacks on the United States], President George W. Bush elevated democratization in the Middle East as a strategic priority. This apt aim, however, was undermined by several factors: the association of democracy promotion with military intervention in Iraq (which did not yield democracy with ease); the use of harsh counterterrorism measures that undercut the symbolism of freedom; the tendency to flinch when likely winners of elections were worrisome (such as in the Palestinian territories); and the failure to meet democracy rhetoric with action in places like Egypt and Pakistan.

The Challenges of the Arab Spring

The protests sweeping the Middle East in early 2011, which have so far caused the ouster of President Zine El Abidine Ben

Ali of Tunisia and rocked the government of President Hosni Mubarak in Egypt, are now confronting President Barack Obama with a familiar challenge. In Egypt, the United States appears to face a classic dilemma: how to handle the potential demise of a friendly autocrat in a strategically important country. On the one hand, President Obama is under pressure to offer more vocal support to those demanding democracy on the streets of Cairo and call for an early change of leadership. On the other, many argue that President Mubarak has protected American interests in the Middle East for thirty years, and there is no guarantee that a new democratic government in Egypt would do the same if the Islamist Muslim Brotherhood should be elected.

President Obama's struggle to reconcile these pressures comes after he began his term distancing himself from Washington's mixed democracy-promotion legacy. His failure to embrace Iran's inspiring Green Movement in the summer of 2009—presumably to keep a door open for dialogue on Iran's nuclear program—was a clear indication of the Obama administration's more realist turn. Now several signals indicate greater comfort with the bipartisan democracy consensus of the Reagan, Clinton, and George W. Bush presidencies. These include President Obama's 2009 Nobel laureate address; Secretary of State Hillary Rodham Clinton's unveiling of another U.S. fund to help besieged human rights defenders; and President Obama's 2010 address to the UN General Assembly, where he said, "There is no right more fundamental than the ability to choose your leaders and determine your destiny." A record of implementation now needs to follow these public statements, whether in Egypt or any number of countries where democracy is absent or at risk—and where long-term U.S. interests are abundantly at stake.

Questions of Means

These historical legacies help highlight the central questions of how to promote democracy. First, is democracy most legitimately and effectively achieved through U.S. or multilateral action? At times, this might prove to be a false choice. If the action of the United States (or another power) is truly in the service of the consent of the governed, rule of law, and fundamental freedoms as understood in the UN charter, then it ought not be rejected out of hand. Yet multilateral action has more perceived legitimacy.

Second, is the use of military force or covert action justified to promote democracy? Sometimes military action may be necessary not just to facilitate or restore democracy, but to end a particularly inhumane form of autocracy. Military intervention in Rwanda in 1994 to prevent or stop genocide would have been just such a case. However, intervention should be a truly last resort.

As for covert activity, the United States conducted secret operations to help forces of democracy in Western Europe early in the Cold War and in Eastern Europe later. Some covert action was justified as promoting democracy when it was merely promoting anti-Soviet actors. Using transparent means to support democratization is best whenever possible.

One effective alternative to direct intervention that the United States has pursued is to engage and support civil society around the world. For a quarter century, operated separately from the U.S. government and working through affiliates of the Democratic Party, Republican Party, Chamber of Commerce, and AFL-CIO [American Federation of Labor and Congress of Industrial Organizations], the National Endowment for Democracy has assisted civil society actors to establish or consolidate democracy all over the world. In addition, private foundations, often in partnership with government, have funded grassroots organizations to help build civil societies globally as well. Support for indigenous, locally led movements is better than direct U.S. government action, whether civilian, military, or covert.

In the past five years, the United Nations has gone further in actively promoting civil society. In 2006, Secretary-General Kofi A. Annan launched the UN Democracy Fund (UNDEF) to support an array of civil society organizations. Eighty-five percent of the funds are required to go to nongovernmental organizations rather than UN agencies or governments as implementers. Prior to UNDEF, a great deal of dialogue occurred in the UN about the importance of civil society to economic development and human rights, but the rhetoric was unmatched by empowering programming. UNDEF is beginning to change that. To date, its four rounds of grants have wisely funded a broad range of democracy's building blocks, including women's empowerment, civic education, and anti-corruption measures. Although UNDEF remains underfunded, it is a step in the right direction. President Obama was right to note in his 2010 address to the UN General Assembly that "it's time for every Member State . . . to increase the UN Democracy Fund."

U.S. enthusiasm for democracy promotion has been shaken in recent years due to a number of political and economic setbacks. These include the turmoil in post-invasion Iraq, election results favoring extremists, growing doubts about the neoliberal economic model, and the rise of an alternative Chinese statist model. Yet the need for democracy is as great as ever, and the most effective means to encourage it are in plain sight.

> "Some may disagree, but I believe America is exceptional—in part because we have shown a willingness through the sacrifice of blood and treasure to stand up not only for our own narrow self-interests, but for the interests of all."

The United States Has a Vital Role in Securing World Peace

Barack Obama

Barack Obama is the forty-fourth president of the United States. In the following viewpoint, he reviews some of the recent international challenges that have tested the United Nations, particularly the unrest in Egypt and Iraq, and he asserts that these situations can be resolved with the support of the international community. President Obama reiterates the US commitment to play a leadership role in that effort, especially when it comes to encouraging democratic reform, ensuring human rights, and securing world peace. It is more important than ever that the United States plays a key role in world affairs and vows to approach new challenges with humility and pragmatism. In that

Barack Obama, "Remarks by President Obama in Address to the United Nations General Assembly," Whitehouse.gov, September 24, 2013.

vein, Obama encourages other nations and international security organizations to take a vital leadership role if the situation warrants in the pursuit of peace and stability.

As you read, consider the following questions:

1. According to President Obama, how many Americans were serving in Iraq and Afghanistan in 2008?

2. According to the viewpoint, what Egyptian leader was democratically elected but unwilling to govern in a way that was fully inclusive?

3. What country does Obama say was threatened by the terrorist group al Qaeda and liberated by a French intervention that was supported by the United States?

Mr. President, Mr. Secretary General, fellow delegates, ladies and gentlemen: Each year we come together to reaffirm the founding vision of this institution [the United Nations]. For most of recorded history, individual aspirations were subject to the whims of tyrants and empires. Divisions of race and religion and tribe were settled through the sword and the clash of armies. The idea that nations and peoples could come together in peace to solve their disputes and advance a common prosperity seemed unimaginable.

The Role of the United Nations

It took the awful carnage of two world wars to shift our thinking. The leaders who built the United Nations were not naïve; they did not think this body could eradicate all wars. But in the wake of millions dead and continents in rubble, and with the development of nuclear weapons that could annihilate a planet, they understood that humanity could not survive the course it was on. And so they gave us this institution, believing that it could allow us to resolve conflicts, enforce rules of behavior, and build habits of cooperation that would grow stronger over time.

For decades, the United Nations has in fact made a difference—from helping to eradicate disease, to educating children, to brokering peace. But like every generation of leaders, we face new and profound challenges, and this body continues to be tested. The question is whether we possess the wisdom and the courage, as nation-states and members of an international community, to squarely meet those challenges; whether the United Nations can meet the tests of our time.

For much of my tenure as president, some of our most urgent challenges have revolved around an increasingly integrated global economy, and our efforts to recover from the worst economic crisis of our lifetime. Now, five years after the global economy collapsed, and thanks to coordinated efforts by the countries here today, jobs are being created, global financial systems have stabilized, and people are once again being lifted out of poverty. But this progress is fragile and unequal, and we still have work to do together to assure that our citizens can access the opportunities that they need to thrive in the 21st century.

Together, we've also worked to end a decade of war. Five years ago, nearly 180,000 Americans were serving in harm's way, and the war in Iraq was the dominant issue in our relationship with the rest of the world. Today, all of our troops have left Iraq. Next year [2014], an international coalition will end its war in Afghanistan, having achieved its mission of dismantling the core of al Qaeda that attacked us on 9/11 [referring to September 11, 2001].

U.S. Challenges

For the United States, these new circumstances have also meant shifting away from a perpetual war footing. Beyond bringing our troops home, we have limited the use of drones so they target only those who pose a continuing, imminent threat to the United States where capture is not feasible, and there is a near certainty of no civilian casualties. We're transferring detainees to other countries and trying terrorists in courts of law, while working diligently to close the prison at Guantánamo Bay. And just as we reviewed how we deploy our extraordinary military capabilities in a way that lives up to our ideals, we've begun to review the way that we gather intelligence, so that we properly balance the legitimate security concerns of our citizens and allies with the privacy concerns that all people share.

As a result of this work, and cooperation with allies and partners, the world is more stable than it was five years ago. But even a glance at today's headlines indicates that dangers remain. In Kenya, we've seen terrorists target innocent civilians in a crowded shopping mall, and our hearts go out to the families of those who have been affected. In Pakistan, nearly 100 people were recently killed by suicide bombers outside a church. In Iraq, killings and car bombs continue to be a terrible part of life. And meanwhile, al Qaeda has splintered into regional networks and militias, which doesn't give them the capacity at this point to carry out attacks like 9/11, but does pose serious threats to governments and diplomats, businesses and civilians all across the globe.

Just as significantly, the convulsions in the Middle East and North Africa have laid bare deep divisions within societies, as an old order is upended and people grapple with what comes next. Peaceful movements have too often been answered by violence—from those resisting change and from extremists trying to hijack change. Sectarian conflict has reemerged. And the potential spread of weapons of mass destruction continues to cast a shadow over the pursuit of peace. . . .

A New Era

When peaceful transitions began in Tunisia and Egypt, the entire world was filled with hope. And although the United States—like others—was struck by the speed of transition, and although we did not—and in fact could not—dictate events, we chose to support those who called for change. And we did so based on the belief that while these transitions will be hard and take time, societies based upon democracy and openness and the dignity of the individual will ultimately be more stable, more prosperous, and more peaceful.

Over the last few years, particularly in Egypt, we've seen just how hard this transition will be. Mohamed Morsi was democratically elected, but proved unwilling or unable to govern in a way that was fully inclusive. The interim government that replaced him responded to the desires of millions of Egyptians who believed the revolution had taken a wrong turn, but it, too, has made decisions inconsistent with inclusive democracy—through an emergency law, and restrictions on the press and civil society and opposition parties.

Of course, America has been attacked by all sides of this internal conflict, simultaneously accused of supporting the Muslim Brotherhood, and engineering their removal of power. In fact, the United States has purposely avoided choosing sides. Our overriding interest throughout these past few years has been to encourage a government that legitimately reflects the will of the Egyptian people, and recognizes true democracy as requiring a respect for minority rights and the rule of law, freedom of speech and assembly, and a strong civil society.

That remains our interest today. And so, going forward, the United States will maintain a constructive relationship with the interim government that promotes core interests like the Camp David Accords and counterterrorism. We'll continue support in areas like education that directly benefit the Egyptian people. But we have not proceeded with the delivery of certain military systems, and our support will depend upon Egypt's progress in pursuing a more democratic path.

Universal Values

And our approach to Egypt reflects a larger point: The United States will at times work with governments that do not meet, at least in our view, the highest international expectations, but who work with us on our core interests. Nevertheless, we will not stop asserting principles that are consistent with our ideals, whether that means opposing the use of violence as a means of suppressing dissent, or supporting the principles embodied in the Universal Declaration of Human Rights.

We will reject the notion that these principles are simply Western exports, incompatible with Islam or the Arab World. We believe they are the birthright of every person. And while we recognize that our influence will at times be limited, although we will be wary of efforts to impose democracy through military force, and although we will at times be accused of hypocrisy and inconsistency, we will be engaged in the region for the long haul. For the hard work of forging freedom and democracy is the task of a generation.

And this includes efforts to resolve sectarian tensions that continue to surface in places like Iraq, Bahrain and Syria. We understand such long-standing issues cannot be solved by outsiders; they must be addressed by Muslim communities themselves. But we've seen grinding conflicts come to an end before—most recently in Northern Ireland, where Catholics and Protestants finally recognized that an endless cycle of conflict was causing both communities to fall behind a fast-moving world. And so we believe those same sectarian conflicts can be overcome in the Middle East and North Africa.

The U.S. Role in the World

To summarize, the United States has a hard-earned humility when it comes to our ability to determine events inside other countries. The notion of American empire may be useful propaganda, but it isn't borne out by America's current policy or by public opinion. Indeed, as recent debates within the United

States over Syria clearly show, the danger for the world is not an America that is too eager to immerse itself in the affairs of other countries or to take on every problem in the region as its own. The danger for the world is that the United States, after a decade of war—rightly concerned about issues back home, aware of the hostility that our engagement in the region has engendered throughout the Muslim world—may disengage, creating a vacuum of leadership that no other nation is ready to fill.

I believe such disengagement would be a mistake. I believe America must remain engaged for our own security. But I also believe the world is better for it. Some may disagree, but I believe America is exceptional—in part because we have shown a willingness through the sacrifice of blood and treasure to stand up not only for our own narrow self-interests, but for the interests of all.

I must be honest, though. We're far more likely to invest our energy in those countries that want to work with us, that invest in their people instead of a corrupt few; that embrace a vision of society where everyone can contribute—men and women, Shia or Sunni, Muslim, Christian or Jew. Because from Europe to Asia, from Africa to the Americas, nations that have persevered on a democratic path have emerged more prosperous, more peaceful, and more invested in upholding our common security and our common humanity. And I believe that the same will hold true for the Arab world.

Confronting New Challenges

This leads me to a final point. There will be times when the breakdown of societies is so great, the violence against civilians so substantial that the international community will be called upon to act. This will require new thinking and some very tough choices. While the United Nations was designed to prevent wars between states, increasingly we face the challenge of preventing slaughter within states. And these challenges will grow more pronounced as we are confronted with states that are fragile or failing—places where horrendous violence can put innocent men, women and children at risk, with no hope of protection from their national institutions.

I have made it clear that even when America's core interests are not directly threatened, we stand ready to do our part to prevent mass atrocities and protect basic human rights. But we cannot and should not bear that burden alone. In Mali, we supported both the French intervention that successfully pushed back al Qaeda, and the African forces who are keeping the peace. In Eastern Africa, we are working with partners to bring the Lord's Resistance Army to an end. And in Libya, when the Security Council provided a mandate to protect civilians, America joined a coalition that took action. Because of what we did there, countless lives were saved, and a tyrant could not kill his way back to power.

Libya

I know that some now criticize the action in Libya as an object lesson. They point to the problems that the country now confronts—a democratically elected government struggling to provide security; armed groups, in some places extremists, ruling parts of a fractured land. And so these critics argue that any intervention to protect civilians is doomed to fail—look at Libya. No one is more mindful of these problems than I am, for they resulted in the death of four outstanding U.S. citizens who were committed to the Libyan people, including Ambassador Chris Stevens—a man whose courageous efforts helped save the city of Benghazi. But does anyone truly believe that the situation in Libya would be better if [Muammar] Gaddafi had been allowed to kill, imprison, or brutalize his people into submission? It's far more likely that without international action, Libya would now be engulfed in civil war and bloodshed.

Barack Obama

Barack Obama is the forty-fourth and current president of the United States and the first African American to hold the office. A Democratic senator from Illinois at the time of his election in November of 2008, Obama prevailed after a grueling primary season against his chief Democratic rival, Senator Hillary Clinton, and a hard-fought presidential campaign against the Republican candidate, Senator John McCain. Obama electrified voters during campaign appearances with a unifying message of hope and an ambitious agenda of change that included ending the war in Iraq and extending affordable health care to all Americans. In his inaugural address on January 20, 2009, he proclaimed: "On this day, we gather because we have chosen hope over fear, unity of purpose over conflict and discord. . . . The time has come to reaffirm our enduring spirit; to choose our better history; to carry forward that precious gift, that noble idea, passed on from generation to generation: the God-given promise that all are equal, all are free, and all deserve a chance to pursue their full measure of happiness." Obama's presidential challenges included the health care debate, a struggling economy, the continuing need for national security and border safety during a time of war, and an oil spill that endangered the wildlife, jobs, and culture of America's Gulf states. Obama was reelected on November 6, 2012.

"Barack Obama," Biography in Context.
Detroit, MI: Gale, 2014.

We live in a world of imperfect choices. Different nations will not agree on the need for action in every instance, and the principle of sovereignty is at the center of our international order. But sovereignty cannot be a shield for tyrants to commit wanton murder, or an excuse for the international community to turn a blind eye. While we need to be modest in our belief that we can remedy every evil, while we need to be mindful that the world is full of unintended consequences, should we really accept the notion that the world is powerless in the face of a Rwanda or Srebrenica? If that's the world that people want to live in, they should say so and reckon with the cold logic of mass graves.

A Global Effort

But I believe we can embrace a different future. And if we don't want to choose between inaction and war, we must get better—all of us—at the policies that prevent the breakdown of basic order. Through respect for the responsibilities of nations and the rights of individuals. Through meaningful sanctions for those who break the rules. Through dogged diplomacy that resolves the root causes of conflict, not merely its aftermath. Through development assistance that brings hope to the marginalized. And yes, sometimes—although this will not be enough—there are going to be moments where the international community will need to acknowledge that the multilateral use of military force may be required to prevent the very worst from occurring.

Ultimately, this is the international community that America seeks—one where nations do not covet the land or resources of other nations, but one in which we carry out the founding purpose of this institution and where we all take responsibility. A world in which the rules established out of the horrors of war can help us resolve conflicts peacefully and prevent the kinds of wars that our forefathers fought. A world where human beings can live with dignity and meet their basic needs, whether they live in New York or Nairobi, in Peshawar or Damascus.

These are extraordinary times, with extraordinary opportunities. Thanks to human progress, a child born anywhere on Earth today can do things today that 60 years ago would have been out of reach for the mass of humanity. I saw this in Africa, where nations moving beyond conflict are now poised to take off. And America is with them, partnering to feed the hungry and care for the sick, and to bring power to places off the grid.

I see it across the Pacific region, where hundreds of millions have been lifted out of poverty in a single generation. I see it in the faces of young people everywhere who can access the entire world with the click of a button, and who are eager to join the cause of eradicating extreme poverty, and combating climate change, starting businesses, expanding freedom, and leaving behind the old ideological battles of the past. That's what's happening in Asia and Africa. It's happening in Europe and across the Americas. That's the future that the people of the Middle East and North Africa deserve as well—one where they can focus on opportunity, instead of whether they'll be killed or repressed because of who they are or what they believe.

Time and again, nations and people have shown our capacity to change—to live up to humanity's highest ideals, to choose our better history. Last month [August 2013], I stood where 50 years ago Martin Luther King Jr. told America about his dream, at a time when many people of my race could not even vote for president. Earlier this year, I stood in the small cell where Nelson Mandela endured decades cut off from his own people and the world. Who are we to believe that today's challenges cannot be overcome, when we have seen what changes the human spirit can bring? Who in this hall can argue that the future belongs to those who seek to repress that spirit, rather than those who seek to liberate it?

I know what side of history I want the United States of America to be on. We're ready to meet tomorrow's challenges with you—firm in the belief that all men and women are in fact created equal, each individual possessed with a dignity and inalienable rights that cannot be denied. That is why we look to the future not with fear, but with hope. And that's why we remain convinced that this community of nations can deliver a more peaceful, prosperous and just world to the next generation.

| "No one appointed the United States the world's policeman."

The United States Should Not Be the World's Policeman

Sheldon Richman

Sheldon Richman is an author, political commentator, and editor of the monthly journal Future of Freedom. *In the following viewpoint, he derides the recent US accusations against Syria, contending that not only should people be skeptical of US allegations that Syria used chemical weapons against its own people but also that the United States has no right to act as if it is the world's policeman. Richman charges the United States of acting like a bully in international affairs—behavior that makes enemies and turns global public opinion against America. Acting as the world's policeman, Richman argues, betrays American values and endangers national security.*

As you read, consider the following questions:

1. Who does Richman identify as the leader of Syria?

2. According to the author, what violent Middle East dictator was supported by the United States after he used chemical weapons on his own people in the 1980s?

Sheldon Richman, "We Must Not Be the World's Policeman," Future of Freedom Foundation, September 4, 2013. Copyright © 2013 by The Future of Freedom Foundation. All rights reserved. Reproduced by permission.

3. What two Middle Eastern dictators does Richman report learned a hard lesson when they crossed the United States in recent years?

Even if everything Secretary of State John Kerry says about chemical weapons in Syria were true, the evidence would prove only that Bashar al-Assad committed crimes against civilians. It would not prove that the U.S. government has either the moral or legal authority to commit acts of war.

These issues must be kept separate. We have reason to be skeptical of Kerry's case—why did President [Barack] Obama try to stop the UN [United Nations] inspection?—but if it were otherwise, the case for U.S. military intervention still would not have been made—even if authorized by Congress.

No one appointed the United States the world's policeman. The government's founding document, the Constitution, does not and could not do so. Obama and Kerry have tried hard to invoke "national security" as grounds for bombing Syria, but no one believes Assad threatens Americans. He has made no such statements and taken no threatening actions. He is engulfed in a sectarian civil war. Inexcusably, Obama has taken sides in that civil war—the same side as the Syrian al-Qaeda affiliate—but still Assad poses no danger to Americans. Bombing would make him more—not less—of a threat.

America as Bully

As it interferes in other people's conflicts, a self-appointed world policeman will breed resentment and a lust for revenge. No one likes a bully, especially when it's a presumptuous superpower armed with nuclear warheads and monstrous conventional weapons. (By the way, Assad's conventional weapons have killed far more people than sarin gas has.)

You might ask, How could U.S. punishment of Assad be equated with being a bully? Isn't *he* the bully? To be sure, Assad is a criminal. But the U.S. government's record on the world's stage hardly qualifies it for any merit badges. It rails against Assad's brutality, but it backed Iraq's late president Saddam Hussein, even when he used chemical weapons in the 1980s. It condoned the Egyptian military's mowing down of over a thousand street demonstrators after the recent coup, and it has more than tacitly approved Israel's string of on-slaughts against the Palestinians and Lebanese. In these cases, American presidents could have properly responded by ending military aid—but they refused.

Similarly, the U.S. government for decades provided advanced weaponry to brutal and corrupt monarchies in the Arab world and autocrats in Asia and Latin America. More often than not, when a government represses its population, it uses equipment made in the USA.

Picking Our Battles

America's selective outrage is not lost on the world. The U.S. government is neither an honest broker nor an avenger of the victims of injustice. It is the world's ham-handed hegemon, with overriding geopolitical and economic interests that determine what it does in any circumstance.

Assad is a suitable foe, not because he is uniquely cruel—hardly—but because Russia and Iran are his allies. American foreign policy in the Middle East has long been dedicated to guaranteeing that no country can challenge U.S./Israeli hegemony. American presidents have no problem with strongmen who crush their people's dreams of freedom, as long as those rulers do what they are told. But if they don't toe the line, watch out. Saddam Hussein and Libya's Muammar Gaddafi learned that the hard way. Now it's Assad's turn (earlier in the "war on terror," the CIA [Central Intelligence Agency] outsourced torture services to him), even if that means helping al-Qaeda in Syria. . . .

No one appointed the United States the world's policeman. By assuming that role, the U.S. government—no matter who's president—undermines the values we claim to uphold, such as freedom, justice, privacy, and peace. The invasions of Iraq and Afghanistan left hundreds of thousands dead, many more gravely wounded, and corrupt authoritarian governments in control of the social wreckage. The law of unintended consequences cannot be repealed, and the risk is no less with interventions that begin modestly, because no one can say what the other side—which includes Iran and Russia—will do.

At home, a perpetual war footing drains our pockets, puts us at risk of retaliation, violates our privacy, and distorts our economy through the military-industrial complex.

James Madison understood well: "No nation could preserve its freedom in the midst of continual warfare."

Periodical and Internet Sources Bibliography

The following articles have been selected to supplement the diverse views presented in this chapter.

John R. Bolton	"Obama's Foreign Policy Based on Belief That Weaker U.S. Is Key to Peace," *Washington Times*, January 27, 2014.
Dennis Byrne	"Obama's Clueless Foreign Policy," *Chicago Tribune*, August 5, 2014.
Liu Chang	"Commentary: Western Interventionism to Blame for Deadly Chaos in Middle East," Xinhua, August 5, 2014.
Dilip Hiro	"Why Won't Anyone Listen to the World's Sole Superpower?," *Mother Jones*, September 30, 2013.
Charles Hurt	"Obama's 'Empty Chair Diplomacy' on 'View,'" *Washington Times*, September 25, 2012.
Hamza Jehangir	"Realism, Liberalism, and the Possibilities of Peace," *E-International Relations*, February 19, 2012.
Robert O. Keohane	"Hegemony and After," *Foreign Affairs*, July–August 2012.
Kevin Placek	"The Democratic Peace Theory," *E-International Relations*, February 18, 2012.
Julia Schemmer	"The First Step to World Peace," *Huffington Post*, January 31, 2014.
Marion Smith	"What Is America's Role in the World?," Heritage Foundation, November 16, 2010.
Dai Xu	"Vigorous Eurasian Community Needed to Counter US Hegemonic Ambition," *Global Times*, June 15, 2014.

CHAPTER 3

What Economic, Social, and Political Factors May Lead to World Peace?

Chapter Preface

According to statistics provided by the United Nations Entity for Gender Equality and the Empowerment of Women, also known as UN Women, the number of women in political leadership positions around the world is dismal. Only nine women serve as elected heads of state and fifteen as the heads of their nations' governments. Approximately 22 percent of national governing bodies are made up of women. Moreover, female political representatives make up less than 10 percent of national legislative bodies in thirty-eight nations. All of these statistics must be considered in light of the fact that women are roughly half of the world's population and make up a majority in many countries. Women are clearly underrepresented in political office in most regions around the world.

In some regions, women play a more substantial leadership role in politics. In Nordic countries, which include Norway, Denmark, Sweden, Finland, and Iceland, women make up 42 percent of their nations' houses of parliament. In the rest of Europe, they average around 23 percent of national parliamentary systems. On the other end of the spectrum, women are least represented in Pacific countries (16.2 percent) and in the Middle East and North Africa (16 percent).

In the United States, women hold 101 out of a total of 535 seats in the 114th Congress. That means that less than one-fifth of Congress is composed of women. Twenty of those women serve in the Senate, representing 20 percent of that chamber. In the House of Representatives, 81 out of 435 seats are held by women. America now ranks ninety-eighth in the world for percentage of women in its national legislature.

The statistics are not much better for state offices. In 2014 only five women had been elected as governors of US states.

When looking at all statewide elective executive offices across the country, 72 out of 318 positions were held by women, or 22.6 percent.

A number of studies show that having robust female participation in political leadership is beneficial to all segments of society. Besides the obvious fact that it is more representative of the population at large, more women in leadership positions would likely lead to greater attention to social and economic inequality, education and health care reform, the protection of human rights and civil liberties, environmental protection and sustainability, and policies that economically support families and individuals. Increasing female leadership in politics would bring more attention to issues that cause societal instability.

Many Americans believe that having more women in leadership positions—in business and in politics—is essential to keeping the United States a world power and beacon for other countries around the globe. "Renewing America's vitality at home and strengthening our leadership abroad will take the energy and talents of all our people, women and men," suggested former US senator and secretary of state Hillary Clinton during a 2013 speech on women's leadership. "If America is going to lead, we need to learn from the women of the world who have blazed new paths and developed new solutions, on everything from economic development to education to environmental protection."

The connection between women's leadership and world peace is one of the topics explored in the following chapter, which considers economic, social, and political movements that can enhance the chances for global harmony. Other viewpoints in the chapter examine the role of free trade, inner peace, gender equality, and religious leadership as contributors to a more peaceful world.

> "Trade helps to humanize the people
> that you trade with. And it's tougher to
> want to go to war with your human
> trading partners than with a country
> you see only as lines on a map."

Free Trade Is an Integral Aspect of World Peace

Julian Adorney

Julian Adorney is a writer and economic historian. In the following viewpoint, he discusses a recent study that reinforces the belief that free trade between countries reduces international conflict. Adorney attributes this conclusion to the fact that free trade forges bonds between nations by humanizing trading partners and facilitating greater understanding and cooperation. Free trade also provides an incentive for peace between trading partners because nations are less likely to go to war with an economic ally. Furthermore, there is evidence that protectionist policies increase hostility between trading partners. Adorney explains that the study finds that although democracy is also a factor in peaceful relations between nations, trade is even more effective in ensuring peace.

As you read, consider the following questions:

1. How does the author define a dyad in the context of Patrick J. McDonald's study?

2. According to the author, what is the Richardson process of reciprocal and increasing hostilities?

3. According to McDonald's analysis, how much would the probability of future conflict decrease if a country from the top 10 percent of protectionist countries is taken to the bottom 10 percent?

Frédéric Bastiat [a nineteenth-century French economist] famously claimed that "if goods don't cross borders, soldiers will."

Bastiat argued that free trade between countries could reduce international conflict because trade forges connections between nations and gives each country an incentive to avoid war with its trading partners. If every nation were an economic island, the lack of positive interaction created by trade could leave more room for conflict. Two hundred years after Bastiat, libertarians take this idea as gospel. Unfortunately, not everyone does. But as recent research shows, the historical evidence confirms Bastiat's famous claim.

To Trade or to Raid

In "Peace Through Trade or Free Trade?" professor Patrick J. McDonald, from the University of Texas at Austin, empirically tested whether greater levels of protectionism in a country (tariffs, quotas, etc.) would increase the probability of international conflict in that nation. He used a tool called dyads to analyze every country's international relations from 1960 until 2000. A dyad is the interaction between one country and another country: German and French relations would be one dyad, German and Russian relations would be a second, French and Australian relations would be a third. He further

111

broke this down into dyad-years; the relations between Germany and France in 1965 would be one dyad-year, the relations between France and Australia in 1973 would be a second, and so on.

Using these dyad-years, McDonald analyzed the behavior of every country in the world for the past 40 years. His analysis showed a negative correlation between free trade and conflict: The more freely a country trades, the fewer wars it engages in. Countries that engage in free trade are less likely to invade and less likely to be invaded.

The Causal Arrow

Of course, this finding might be a matter of confusing correlation for causation. Maybe countries engaging in free trade fight less often for some other reason, like the fact that they tend also to be more democratic. Democratic countries make war less often than empires do. But McDonald controls for these variables. Controlling for a state's political structure is important, because democracies and republics tend to fight less than authoritarian regimes.

McDonald also controlled for a country's economic growth, because countries in a recession are more likely to go to war than those in a boom, often in order to distract their people from their economic woes. McDonald even controlled for factors like geographic proximity: It's easier for Germany and France to fight each other than it is for the United States and China, because troops in the former group only have to cross a shared border.

The takeaway from McDonald's analysis is that protectionism can actually lead to conflict. McDonald found that a country in the bottom 10 percent for protectionism (meaning it is less protectionist than 90 percent of other countries) is 70 percent less likely to engage in a new conflict (either as invader or as target) than one in the top 10 percent for protectionism.

"You come to bring us peace and brotherhood? — Could we just have the money instead?"

© Baloo/Rex May/Cartoonstock.com.

Protectionism and War

Why does protectionism lead to conflict, and why does free trade help to prevent it? The answers, though well known to classical liberals, are worth mentioning.

First, trade creates international goodwill. If Chinese and American businessmen trade on a regular basis, both sides benefit. And mutual benefit disposes people to look for the good in each other. Exchange of goods also promotes an exchange of cultures. For decades, Americans saw China as a mysterious country with strange, even hostile values. But in the 21st century, trade between our nations has increased markedly, and both countries know each other a little better now. iPod-wielding Chinese teenagers are like American teenagers, for example. They're not terribly mysterious. Likewise, the Chinese understand democracy and American consumerism more than they once did. The countries may not find overlap in all of each other's values, but trade has helped us to at least understand each other.

Trade helps to humanize the people that you trade with. And it's tougher to want to go to war with your human trading partners than with a country you see only as lines on a map.

Second, trade gives nations an economic incentive to avoid war. If Nation X sells its best steel to Nation Y, and its businessmen reap plenty of profits in exchange, then businessmen on both sides are going to oppose war. This was actually the case with Germany and France right before World War I. Germany sold steel to France, and German businessmen were firmly opposed to war. They only grudgingly came to support it when German ministers told them that the war would only last a few short months. German steel had a strong incentive to oppose war, and if the situation had progressed a little differently—or if the German government had been a little more realistic about the timeline of the war—that incentive might have kept Germany out of World War I.

Third, protectionism promotes hostility. This is why free trade, not just aggregate trade (which could be accompanied by high tariffs and quotas), leads to peace. If the United States imposes a tariff on Japanese automobiles, that tariff hurts Japanese businesses. It creates hostility in Japan toward the United States. Japan might even retaliate with a tariff on U.S. steel, hurting U.S. steel makers and angering our government, which would retaliate with another tariff. Both countries now have an excuse to leverage nationalist feelings to gain support at home; that makes outright war with the other country an easier sell, should it come to that.

In socioeconomic academic circles, this is called the Richardson process of reciprocal and increasing hostilities; the United States harms Japan, which retaliates, causing the United States to retaliate again. History shows that the Richardson process can easily be applied to protectionism. For instance, in the 1930s, industrialized nations raised tariffs and trade barriers; countries eschewed multilateralism and turned inward. These decisions led to rising hostilities, which helped set World War II in motion.

These factors help explain why free trade leads to peace, and protectionism leads to more conflict.

Free Trade and Peace

One final note: McDonald's analysis shows that taking a country from the top 10 percent for protectionism to the bottom 10 percent will reduce the probability of future conflict by 70 percent. He performed the same analysis for the democracy of a country and showed that taking a country from the top 10 percent (very democratic) to the bottom 10 percent (not democratic) would only reduce conflict by 30 percent.

Democracy is a well-documented deterrent: The more democratic a country becomes, the less likely it is to resort to international conflict. But reducing protectionism, according to McDonald, is more than twice as effective at reducing conflict than becoming more democratic.

Here in the United States, we talk a lot about spreading democracy. We invaded Iraq partly to "spread democracy." A *New York Times* op-ed by Professor Dov Ronen of Harvard University claimed that "the United States has been waging an ideological campaign to spread democracy around the world" since 1989. One of the justifications for our international crusade is to make the world a safer place.

Perhaps we should spend a little more time spreading free trade instead. That might really lead to a more peaceful world.

> "One consequence of the view of
> women's roles in war as primarily pas-
> sive victims is that little thought is
> given to the role women ought to play
> in the reintegration of combatants into
> the societies from which they came."

The Role of Women in Global Security

Valerie Norville

Valerie Norville is the director of publications for the United States Institute of Peace. In the following viewpoint, she outlines efforts to recognize the vital role women play in building durable peace and maintaining security throughout the world. Norville identifies three areas in which women's participation could make a significant difference in fostering security: peaceful decision making and peacekeeping; reconciliation, reintegration, and rule of law; and economic development. Despite some advances, women remain woefully underrepresented in leadership positions. As a result, the needs and perspectives of women are often overlooked when it comes to important areas. Norville enumerates several ways to increase women's participation in leadership roles.

As you read, consider the following questions:

1. According to Norville, for what did United Nations Security Council resolution 1325 call?

2. What three countries does the author cite as ones that implemented quotas on the percentage of women serving in parliament?

3. How many cases of sexual violence does the author report have been documented in the Democratic Republic of the Congo since 1996?

Women are often viewed as victims of conflict. But this view masks the important roles women play as leaders, especially in helping end conflict, developing post-conflict reintegration efforts and economic life, and even in leading the organization of camps for internally displaced persons. Participants at the conference on the role of women in global security identified recommendations for ways to provide assistance, tools, and motivation to encourage women to become such leaders in their communities.

In conflict zones, women are active participants in the conflicts that affect their countries. They may become combatants. They may become the sole providers for their families, more active in the informal or formal sectors of the economy, or more active in peacemaking groups as a result of conflict. They also suffer disproportionately from sexual violence and displacement. Yet during war and in its aftermath, women too often are excluded from activities aimed at resolving the violent conflicts that so deeply affect them.

Those conflicts cannot be brought to a lasting end without making women's lives more secure, and it is women who are best positioned to determine how that security is achieved. This report focuses on three key areas in which women could foster security: peace decision making and peacekeeping; reconciliation, reintegration, and rule of law; and economic development.

Recognizing that sustainable security is not possible without the involvement of women, the United Nations in October 2000 passed Security Council resolution 1325. The resolution calls for increased representation of women at peace negotiations and at all levels of decision making regarding security; inclusion of women in post-conflict reconstruction efforts and in disarmament, demobilization, and reintegration efforts; increased protection from sexual violence; and an end to impunity for crimes affecting women.

> The resolution undergirds the efforts of those advocating for gender equality and greater sensitivity to gender issues, or "gender mainstreaming." Follow-on UN resolutions—particularly 1820, 1888, and 1889—created an office of a special representative for eliminating sexual violence against women, mandated measures of accountability, authorized UN sanctions in these cases, and defined widespread sexual violence itself as a threat to international peace and security. And in October 2010, the UN adopted a plan to monitor progress on implementing 1325.

"We are fortunate that the unique role of women as key contributors to peace and security is growing," said Lene Espersen, Denmark's minister of foreign affairs. "And we already possess substantial knowledge about the critical importance of women in the prevention and resolution of conflicts and in post-conflict reconciliation and reintegration."

Despite these advances, women in zones of conflict and in reconstruction efforts, and those working on their behalf, emphasize that they often have little or no voice in negotiating peace or planning reconstruction, lack economic opportunities, and continue to be the primary targets of ongoing sexual violence. It is therefore critical to pool the knowledge of those working on issues of gender equality and inclusion to determine what measures and practices have proved effective or ought to be tried in countries emerging from war.

To that end, three hundred military, diplomatic, academic, nongovernmental organizations (NGO), the United Nations, and business sector experts at a 2010 conference in Copenhagen on the role of women in global security shared experiences in conflict zones, offered recommendations for ways to increase women's participation in global security, and cited barriers to putting those recommendations in practice. Participants from Afghanistan, Liberia, and Uganda attended, as well as from Europe, the United States, NATO [North Atlantic Treaty Organization], the United Nations and the European Union. Their discussions were organized around three themes: peacemaking and peacekeeping, reconciliation and reconstruction, and economic development.

Peacemaking and Peacekeeping

Women are typically excluded from formal peace processes. They tend to be absent at the peace table, underrepresented in parliaments that are developing policy in countries emerging from conflict, and underrepresented in peacekeeping forces. Melanne Verveer, who heads the State Department's Office of Global Women's Issues, noted that thirty-one of the world's thirty-nine active conflicts represent recurrences of conflict after peace settlements were concluded. In all thirty-one cases, women were excluded from the peace process.

The United Nations reckons that fewer than 3 percent of signatories to peace agreements have been women and that women's participation in peace negotiations averages less than 8 percent for the eleven peace processes for which such information is available. Such agreements typically do not address sexual violence.

Rosalba Oywa, executive director of the People's Voice for Peace in Gulu, a Ugandan NGO, makes clear that exclusion of women is not due to a lack of women's desire or ability to be active in negotiations. She cites her experience in Uganda, where the Ugandan government and the Lord's Resistance

Army (LRA) engaged in a brutal conflict characterized by abductions of thousands of girls and boys by the LRA, displacement, and widespread rape and other atrocities. "Women activists and women-led organizations mobilized to lead not
only peacebuilding at the community level but to play a direct
role in finding a negotiated settlement," Oywa said. During
peace talks to end the war in northern Uganda, women
marched hundreds of miles, from Uganda to the site of the
talks in Juba, Sudan, to press for observer status at the talks,
but they played no direct role in the negotiations.

Likewise, women in Liberia were not invited to peace negotiations with the rebel groups in 2003. But, added Liberia's
minister of gender and development, Vabah Gayflor, "Women
made their voices heard by sheer will," marching, praying, and
singing at the site of negotiations. Women were subsequently
mobilized to give support to national elections that led to
Ellen Johnson Sirleaf becoming president of Liberia. The momentum built during those efforts continues, she said, as rural
women take leadership in farm cooperatives and managing
microcredit groups to help reduce rural poverty.

Even in the difficult circumstances of refugee camps,
women have demonstrated an ability to organize, lead, and
communicate the needs of other women in the camps, said
Maria Otero, undersecretary for democracy and global affairs
at the U.S. State Department. With this input, international
groups can provide responsive, practical tools for women's
protection, such as water purification tablets and cookstoves,
which have proved critical in reducing the amount of time
women spend gathering wood, the resultant environmental
harm, and their exposure to violence, she said.

Representation in parliament is also critical to ensuring
that women's concerns are taken into account in countries rebuilding after war. Although there is debate about whether
quotas are the best means to achieve increased representation,
many experts believe quotas are essential, and they have been

instituted in several countries, including Uganda (where women constitute 31.5 percent of the legislature), Rwanda (56 percent of the lower house), and Afghanistan (27.5 percent in the upper house).

Betty Amongi, a member of Uganda's Parliament, ran for office in 2001 as an independent determined to help bring peace to northern Uganda, an area where she grew up and one that had seen continuous war throughout her life. She has worked to build a network of women parliamentarians to advocate for an agenda that takes gender into account in Uganda's ongoing reconstruction and reconciliation efforts. For instance, women have pressed strongly for adding maternity wards to planned hospital construction, according to Amongi, and for higher priority for trauma counseling and start-up capital for women to build businesses.

"When you have a critical mass of women in power, legislation tends to get passed that favors women," said Judy Cheng-Hopkins, assistant secretary-general for the UN Peacebuilding Support Office. She cited a rise in health care spending in Rwanda and changes elsewhere to women's ability to own and inherit land and to criminalization of sexual abuse.

Another area for women's participation in peacebuilding lies in peacekeeping operations. Those advocating for increasing the number of women in peacekeeping missions argue that the prospects of sustainable peace are improved by providing those living in conflict areas with positive female role models, facilitating good relations between traumatized civilians and security services, giving authority a female face, and offering an alternative perspective on conflict resolution.

Yet participation of women peacekeepers is negligible. In missions directed by the UN's Department of Peacekeeping Operations, women represented 3 percent of total military contingents in 2010. Low numbers of women acting as military peacekeepers reflect the low overall rates of participation of women in the armed forces of countries that contribute peacekeeping forces. Even in Denmark, one of the first countries to adopt a national action plan to implement resolution 1325, women make up around 5 percent of Danish military forces and a similar percentage in peacekeeping missions. Limited numbers of women recruited overall mean limited numbers available to deploy. Consequently, removing barriers to overall recruitment efforts in troop-contributing countries is seen as key to improved recruitment in peacekeeping, along with more incentives for women to join peacekeeping missions.

Raymond E. Mabus, U.S. secretary of the navy, cited U.S. experience: The military is more likely to retain younger women when they observe older women being promoted to top officer positions. He also pointed to the success of the Marines' experiment with a female engagement team in Afghanistan, where a team of forty women soldiers were deployed for six months this year to meet with women and children, learn about their needs and concerns, and build trust as part of the overall counterinsurgency strategy in the region. The existence of such teams recognizes the importance of local women's perspectives and their influence on local situations, to which the all-male forces in these cultures have limited or no access.

"As the first deployment of the U.S. Marine female engagement team came to an end, one of the commanders of the relieving unit brought all the patrol leaders from the Marine brigade with seven months of experience into a room and asked them what they needed to make the deployment more successful," Mabus said. "He expected the answer to be more guns, more ammunition, or more logistical support, but the number one answer from these young infantry corporals and sergeants was instead more female engagement teams."

Participants also stressed the need for all peacekeeping forces to receive training to make them more aware of the gender dynamics of the conflicts to which they are deployed.

Many also pointed to the salutary effects of joint male-female forces in reducing the potential for sexual abuse of civilians by the peacekeeping troops themselves, as has occurred in several conflict zones.

Reconciliation, Reintegration, and Rule of Law

One consequence of the view of women's roles in war as primarily passive victims is that little thought is given to the role women ought to play in the reintegration of combatants into the societies from which they came. In addition, women's views are typically not incorporated when post-conflict governments set up mechanisms for reconciliation between armed groups and civilians.

But women and girls have played many roles in conflict in different parts of the world, as fighters, supporters of rebel groups, spouses, or slave labor. Women's participation is therefore critical in processes of DDR [disarmament, demobilization, and reintegration], and by excluding them, critical opportunities for rebuilding communities are lost.

DDR is inexorably linked to reform of rule of law, security sector, and justice systems, and in all these areas the needs of women, girls, men, and boys must be taken into account so that government adequately addresses every group's need for protection from ongoing violence.

Uganda's Amongi puts it in stark terms when she asks how justice is to be defined for families in which rebel groups forced sons to rape mothers, and fathers their daughters, before those fathers and sons were abducted and forcibly conscripted. The purpose of this brutal tactic was to prevent conscripts from rejoining the community at a future date, where they knew they would not be welcome. Amongi argues that everyone in the community, including women, has the task of making the tough decisions about how to balance restoration of community life and retribution for crimes committed during the war. Such decisions may include amnesty, more judges at the local level, persuading leaders to set aside land for mothers raising children born of wartime sexual violence, or, as occurred in Uganda, a ritual cleansing of ex-combatant boys to help them shed their roles as perpetrators of atrocities and pave the way for their return to community life. Whatever the choices, participants agreed that successful DDR requires more gender-inclusive, local participation.

Where cases of sexual violence worldwide have been documented (and recognizing the likelihood that many cases are never reported), the numbers are staggering: More than 200,000 cases have been documented in the Democratic Republic of the Congo (DRC) since 1996 and a present daily average of 40 in the DRC province of South Kivu alone, as many as half a million during the 1994 genocide in Rwanda, at least 50,000 in Sierra Leone, and between 20,000 and 50,000 in Bosnia-Herzegovina in the early 1990s. Prosecutions for these crimes have been rare.

In conflicts marked by high levels of sexual and gender-based violence, the end of the conflict may not bring an end to that violence. In the aftermath of some conflicts, sexual violence actually rises as a consequence of a culture of impunity and in the absence of institutions to protect communities and apprehend and try perpetrators. In such settings, women can be prevented from getting education, regaining physical and psychological health, gaining a stable financial footing, and participating in all aspects of governance and peacebuilding.

Some pointed to the role technology can play. "Women have been known to use mobile phones, for instance, to report crimes perpetrated against them and to testify in situations where they would be otherwise unable due to distance and difficulties in traveling," said Juliet Asante, the chief executive officer of Eagle Productions, Ltd., in Ghana.

Women in Leadership Positions

- Only 21.8 per cent of national parliamentarians were female as of 1 July 2013, a slow increase from 11.3 per cent in 1995.

- As of January 2014, 9 women served as head of state and 15 served as head of government.

- Rwanda had the highest number of women parliamentarians worldwide. Women there have won 63.8 per cent of seats in the lower house.

- Globally, there are 38 states in which women account for less than 10 per cent of parliamentarians in single or lower houses, as of January 2014.

- Wide variations remain in the average percentages of women parliamentarians in each region, across all chambers (single, lower and upper houses). As of 1 January 2014, these were: Nordic countries, 42.1 per cent; Americas, 25.2 per cent; Europe excluding Nordic countries, 23.3 per cent; sub-Saharan Africa, 22.5 per cent; Asia, 18.4 per cent; Pacific, 16.2 per cent; and the Middle East and North Africa, 16.0 per cent.

"Facts and Figures: Leadership and Political Participation,"
UN Entity for Gender Equality and
the Empowerment of Women, 2014.

Economic Development

It is widely understood that economic recovery is important for stability in countries transitioning out of conflict. Determining who has access to economic opportunity has important implications for sustainable peace. Because wars create more female heads of households and force more women to become active in informal markets so their families can survive, reconstruction offers countries the opportunity to take a new look at the constraints women face in building businesses. By investing in half of their human capital that is most underutilized, countries that institute gender-aware reforms can also realize important macroeconomic benefits.

A key area for new policy is removing legal constraints, including restrictions on women's ownership of land. Land is one of the more important assets for households in developing countries, but women in these countries are less likely than men to own and control it. Worldwide, women own 1 to 2 percent of registered land. In Uganda, where women are the primary cultivators, women own 7 percent of the land they till. Because they access land through male relatives, women's economic security is weak, and any decisions regarding investment or selling land typically require the signature of a husband or other male relative. Conflict magnifies the difficulties that such legal restrictions place on women, where men may be absent and more women become widows and thus heads of households but cannot inherit the land on which they work.

Another important constraint in post-conflict settings is the difficulty women face in starting businesses. When the Taliban came to power in Afghanistan in 1996 and barred women from public life and work, Afghan women turned to informal enterprises for their livelihoods, and the importance of the informal economy for women continues to the present. The World Bank reports that more than half of Afghan women in female-headed households are sewing, embroidering, or washing laundry for others. As one Afghan participant put it, "Economic activity is critical to the empowerment of women, especially in Afghanistan, where women are confined to the four walls of the house" and where weak, broken, corrupt institutions make it critical to allow women to build enterprises at home.

"Doing business anywhere in the world is difficult, but add conflict and that makes it even more difficult," said Rangina Hamidi, president of Kandahar Treasure, which employs women artisans in Kandahar. The benefits of informal enterprise are manifold, she added. "Instead of depending on the aid world for short-term, ill-visioned projects that are decided outside your community and country, business allows us to own the work we do," and therefore to benefit society and to pay for educating their children.

While expressing admiration for the resilience and creativity of women operating in informal sectors of the economy, many experts call for removing barriers to women's entry into formal enterprises as well. In post-conflict Liberia, half of all enterprises are informal. A Foreign Investment Advisory Service survey of barriers to converting informal businesses to formal ones in Liberia confirmed that women are more likely than men to own informal enterprises, fewer women had taken steps to formalize their enterprises, and those that tried to obtain licenses or permits reported more difficulty in dealing with government officials. Because informal businesses were less likely to experience increased employment, the analysis suggested that the preponderance of informal enterprise was an impediment to business growth.

Limited access to finance and capital is another constraint facing female entrepreneurs, and this constraint becomes more acute during war. Microcredit has proved a key mechanism for helping women in small, informal enterprises, both in building businesses and dignity in difficult circumstances. Unlike traditional finance mechanisms, microfinance takes into account women's inability to use land or other resources as collateral.

"It also means they can begin to plan longer term," said Otero. The ability to save and plan their spending increases the economic security of women.

Conclusions

NATO secretary-general Anders Fogh Rasmussen summed up the themes of the conference:

Women are not just victims of conflict. They must also be part of the solution. If women are not active participants in peacebuilding and reconciliation, the views, needs, and interests of half of the population in a conflict area are not properly represented. That is simply wrong. It can also undermine the peace.... Resolution 1325 is a landmark resolution because it not only recognizes the impact of conflict on women, it also recognizes the important role that women can play—and indeed must play—in preventing and resolving conflict and in building peace.

Verveer added that resolution 1325 "cannot and must not be seen as a favor to women.... Women's exclusion from the peace process undermines the long-term post-conflict transformation that must take place."

According to the United Nations, twenty-three nations have adopted action plans to implement resolution 1325 in the ten years since it was adopted, and several only recently. The United States announced in October 2010 that it will develop a national action plan as well.

To mark resolution 1325's anniversary, the United Nations Security Council in October 2010 declared its support for a report by the secretary-general that includes twenty-six quantitative and qualitative indicators to measure progress on implementing 1325. While citing myriad actions taken over the last decade to increase women's role in global security, the secretary-general's report acknowledged that these efforts have lacked coordination and have been hampered by the lack of measurable results. Conference participants expressed the hope that better data collection efforts would lead to more effective gender equality and mainstreaming in peace and security efforts. The UN's Cheng-Hopkins cited two salient elements of the secretary-general's action plan for implementing 1325: a target of 15 percent of post-conflict spending going to gender-equality efforts and a recommendation that countries that have instituted a quota system for women in parliament share best practices.

Another participant spoke of her own experience with quotas in Afghanistan: "It was mandated [in Helmand province] that five out of the thirty members of the Gereshk Community Council must be women," said Charlotte Brath, a Danish civilian military cooperation officer. "Everyone was skeptical of this idea, even the Danish female officer who was working with them. But it worked. The women were well educated, well respected, and able. Because of these five women role models, more women are now politically and publically active." But, she added, "since I left Helmand province in February 2010, it has not been possible to deploy another female officer to work with the women. When we are so eager to have the Afghan women become more actively involved, why are we so afraid to have more women actively participate ourselves?"

Although the conference workshops parsed the issues of gender and security into their economic, political, justice, and human rights components, many participants stressed the futility of countries, NGOs, and international organizations focusing on only one or two elements, as all components are integral to an effective, whole-of-government approach to increasing security for women. As such, the best practices discussed at the conference are not part of an à la carte menu, but part of one recipe for progress on women's inclusion. For example, there is no way to increase women's participation in the formal economy if it is not safe for them to leave the house, and reconciliation is not possible where a culture of impunity for crimes against women prevails. Yet if women are allowed to take leading roles in reconstruction, peacebuilding, and the economy, they can change the gender dynamics and attitudes of their societies.

"We are often told that women can't be mediators, they can't be negotiators, and they can't play significant roles in the [peace] process because there are no qualified women," Verveer said. "Experience tells us otherwise. Therefore, we need to make sure that when we are told that qualified women are not available, we have lists ready."

Many experts have emphasized that post-conflict environments can offer women a window of opportunity to consolidate wartime gains in entrepreneurial or peacebuilding skills and to redefine traditional gender roles in war's aftermath. Another common theme stressed by those who work on gender and security issues is that the goal of gender-based programs and national action plans is not only to improve women's lives but to affect the relationship between men and women, particularly in fragile societies, where cultural barriers to women's participation in security tend to be high.

"Women and men are both partners and should work hand in hand," said Jani Jallah, youth representative of the Angie Brooks International Centre in Liberia. "In programs that focus on women, at least one day should be dedicated to educating men on the importance of empowering their wives. We have to have a balanced society. If we focus only on women, in the future we will see that we have the problem that more women are educated than men."

Although cultural norms may appear immutable, participants stressed that in many societies struggling for stability after war, power relationships in old regimes and prevailing cultural barriers become more malleable and subject to change.

The key to women taking advantage of the fluid period new regimes may offer is thus to convince government officials and local leaders that involving women is critical to creating lasting peace. As Søren Pind, Danish minister of development cooperation, said, "You won't find a fragile state that supports the rights of women. You won't find a stable society that neglects the rights of women. I believe that the stability and development of a society are directly interlinked with the rights and activities of its women. We must take up the dual challenge of working in fragile states and of pursuing the women, peace, and security agenda."

> "Religious leaders must come together as never before and take an active role in making an interfaith dialogue with global peace and security as its goal."

Religious Leadership Is Conducive to Global Harmony

Mustafa Ceric

Mustafa Ceric is a Bosnian politician, prominent Islamic leader, and president of the World Bosniak Congress. In the following viewpoint, he asserts that religious leadership can be a positive force in bringing about world peace by motivating individuals to strive for justice, tolerance, and compassion. Ceric acknowledges that there have been a number of instances where religion has been used to justify bad behavior. He explains that one key responsibility of religious leaders is to facilitate interfaith dialogue that prioritizes global peace and security. Ceric reviews three recent initiatives that he believes were prime examples of open intellectual exchange between different faith traditions. These three examples show the key role religious leaders can play in the global effort for peace and security.

As you read, consider the following questions:

1. What five events does the author view as the culmination of human madness and irrationality?

2. According to Ceric, how many Muslim senior scholars came together in October 2007 to write "A Common Word Between Us and You"?

3. According to Archbishop Vinko Puljic, how long did the siege of Sarajevo last?

Religion is one of the factors that make up personal and group identities. The question is how can religious identity be saved from being misused to legitimize immoral and inhumane behavior, and be used instead to motivate people to strive for peace, justice, and tolerance in everyday life situations.

Today, we do not live in a separate world of our own. We do not live in silos. We see that within a relatively short period of history, the telephone, radio, film, television, and, more recently, computers, e-mail, Facebook, Twitter, and the World Wide Web are drastically altering our perceptions of time, space, and each other.

However, these tools of modern technology that make people closer in the communications sense, do not live up to their much-needed potential to make people across boundaries closer in the sense of creating decent human relationships. We see that we continue to be far from a peaceful resolution to centuries of bloody ethnic and religious tensions and conflicts. The genocidal and tragic events in Srebrenica of 1995, in New York and Washington of 2001, in Madrid of 2004, in London of 2005, and in Oslo of 2011 are the culmination of human madness and irrationality.

Indeed, the real issue here is morality, whether it be faith in God, or human consciousness, or man's rational ability to differentiate between true and false, right and wrong, good and evil; or, whether it be morality that is based on pure human feeling, taste, urge, wish or whim. . . .

Religious leaders are important factors in shaping group identities as well as individual and collective morality. Therefore, they must work together to stop man "to act as his own destroyer." Religious leaders must come together as never before and take an active role in making an interfaith dialogue with global peace and security as its goal. Among many global initiatives towards peace brought about by world religious leaders that I have participated in, three deserve our mention.

Three Global Initiatives

First, the Muslim initiative of the Common Word. It came on October 13, 2006, as a result of Pope Benedict XVI's Regensburg address of September 13, 2006. Somewhat surprised by the pope's remark about the Prophet Muhammad, 38 Muslim authorities and scholars from around the world, representing all denominations and schools of thought, joined together to deliver an answer to the pope in the spirit of open intellectual exchange and mutual understanding. In their open letter to the pope, Muslim scholars from every branch of Islam spoke with one voice about the true teachings of Islam.

On October 13, 2007, a year after the open letter, Muslims expanded their message. In "A Common Word Between Us and You," 138 Muslim senior scholars (ulama), as well as Muslim academicians, came together to declare common ground between Christianity and Islam. Every major Muslim country or region in the world was represented in this message, which is addressed to the leaders of all the world's churches, and indeed to all Christians everywhere. And the Christian global leaders responded positively to this Muslim initiative.

Second, the Muslim-Christian common action in Nigeria from May 22–26, 2012, which was organized by the Royal Aal al-Bayt Institute [for Islamic Thought] and the World Council of Churches (WCC). This action was proposed in reaction to the numerous incidents of fierce intercommunal strife that affected the lives of Nigerians during 2000–2012. The idea of the joint Christian-Muslim delegation in response to situations of violence involving both religious groups emerged initially from the "A Common Word" global Muslim-Christian initiative of October 2007 and then from a proposal made in November 2010, when a group of some 60 Christian and Muslim leaders met in Geneva, Switzerland, at the WCC headquarters and forged an agreement to work more cooperatively in situations of conflict.

An Outline of Objectives

The objectives of the Christian-Muslim common action in Nigeria were as follows:

1. To fact-find and investigate firsthand, impartially and credibly, the situation on the ground in Nigeria, and the various factors that have led to the present tensions.

2. To express clearly to both the political and religious leadership in Nigeria the concern and anxiety of the international community about the current situation.

3. To demonstrate an international model of Muslims and Christians working together in an interreligious engagement aimed at fostering peace and harmony between people of different religions.

4. To identify areas or projects where religious institutes, persons, texts, messages, or projects can help ameliorate the situation in Nigeria.

A well-documented report issued by the international Christian-Muslim delegation that visited Nigeria pointed to an inadequate depth of understanding of both Christianity and Islam within and without these two religions, and lack of knowledge and information on a popular level, particularly in local languages, of the scriptural-based condemnations of violence and terrorism in both Christianity and Islam.

At the end of the Nigeria visit, the international Muslim-Christian delegation issued a joint press release, saying:

> We hope by our visit to demonstrate an international model of Muslims and Christians working together in interreligious engagement aimed at fostering peace and harmony between people of different religions. We bear witness that we believe that both Christianity and Islam are religions which long for peace, and that in both our faiths love of God and love of our neighbor must belong together.

And third, the interreligious international meetings that started in the mid-80s, as an initiative of the Community of Sant'Egidio, with the aim of promoting mutual understanding and dialogue among religions, in a horizon of peace. The Community of Sant'Egidio has continued living the spirit of the Assisi World Day of Prayer [for Peace], proposed by [Pope] John Paul II in 1986, by accepting the pope's final invitation of that historical meeting: "Let's keep spreading the message of Peace and living the spirit of Assisi."

A Global Peace Effort

Since that moment, through a network of friendship between representatives of different faiths and cultures from more than 60 countries, the community has promoted a pilgrimage of peace, which has had several stages in various European and Mediterranean cities year after year. The most recent of these was held in Sarajevo. This was a good occasion for the Vrhbosna Archbishop Vinko Puljic to remind the world that:

> These days, specifically April 5, 2012—Holy Thursday—mark the 20th anniversary of the tragic war in Bosnia and Herzegovina and of the dramatic siege of the city of Sarajevo.

> It was the longest siege of the 20th century, from April 1992 to February 1996. Four years of violence, suffering, of daily

Religion and Geopolitics

The existence of state religion is the most obvious example of the relationship between religion and politics. A state religion is a religious body or doctrine that is endorsed by the government. Many beliefs that once existed as state religion ... have been largely relegated to the annals of history.

Such state religions as Christianity and Islam have continued into the modern world. Thirteen countries ... and numerous smaller regional governments recognize a form of Christianity as the state religion. Only one nation—the Vatican City—is governed as a Christian theocracy, a form of government in which a religious leader rules as a deity's representative. Two countries ... recognize forms of Buddhism as state religions. The Israeli Declaration of Independence and subsequent legislation declare Israel a "Jewish state," but the documents do not specify whether the term "Jewish" refers to religion or ethnicity. In practice, however, Israeli political life and institutions are closely linked with religion, especially Orthodox Judaism.

Most countries with a majority Muslim population consider Islam as the state religion. Seventeen of these countries recognize Sunni Islam as the state religion. Only Iran has Shia Islam as the state religion. ... Iraq and Pakistan, both of which have large populations of Sunnis and Shiites, list Islam as the state religion without reference to a particular sect. Bahrain, Kuwait, and Yemen recognize both Sunni and Shia Islam as state religions, while Oman recognizes Ibadi Islam.

"Religion and Geopolitics,"
Global Issues in Context Online Collection.
Detroit, MI: Gale, 2014.

bombings . . . a particular noise to which my ears became accustomed, so much so that today I am forced to wear an ear device in order to restore my hearing lost in those days.

Twenty years is still too short to narrate what happened in Sarajevo, which has always been a city of exemplary coexistence between Christians, Jews, and Muslims. But it is also a city of pain and conflict. In a way, Sarajevo encompasses the beginning and the end of every war of the 20th century. It was in Sarajevo, in fact, that the First World War originated. Sarajevo was the theater of the last tragic conflict of the 1900s. Sarajevo, city of suffering and hope. In his historic visit in 1997, Pope John Paul II called Sarajevo the "Jerusalem of Europe." . . .

Hence, the Sarajevo appeal for peace that was signed on September 11, 2012, by a great number of world religious leaders from China, Japan, Asia, Africa, Australia, America, Europe, and the Balkans is worthwhile reading again and again to remind us of the importance of the role of religious leaders for a global peace and security.

The Sarajevo Appeal for Peace

Indeed, this Sarajevo appeal for peace is to remind us of the importance of the peace of Sarajevo, which is known to be the starting place for wars at both the beginning and the end of the 20th century. May God save Sarajevo from any more wars and bless it to be the heart of peace for the whole world, as we read this Sarajevo appeal for peace:

Men and women of different religions, we have gathered at the invitation of the Community of Sant'Egidio and of the Islamic, Orthodox, Catholic, and Jewish communities of Sarajevo. We have gathered in this land, beautiful and wounded by the last war fought in Europe. Many people in Sarajevo remember the sorrows of that conflict. Many people in Sarajevo remind us all that war is a great evil and it leaves a poisoned legacy behind. With all our strength, we must avoid sliding into the dreadful spiral of hatred, violence, and war. Neighbors must never find themselves fighting against each other because they belong to different religions or ethnic groups. Never again in this land! Never again in this world!

We asked ourselves whether coexistence with people of different religions or ethnic groups bears in itself the seeds of hatred and violence. No, this must not be. Even though, unfortunately, too many countries suffer because of violence, war, and insecurity. In our times different people increasingly become closer to one another geographically. However, this is not enough. We need to become close to each other intimately. We need to do so spiritually, though our differences in terms of religion remain.

We are different. But our unanimous conviction is this: living together is possible, all over the world, and it bears much fruit. It is possible in Sarajevo and everywhere. The future must be prepared with responsibility. And religions have a great responsibility in this respect. In these days in Sarajevo we have lived the grace of dialogue and seen how to build the future.

Today, however, in a time of economic crisis, the temptation to withdraw into oneself is strong, or even to blame other peoples for one's problems, whether past or present. A people then turn into an alien, even into an enemy. Dangerous cultures of resentment, hatred, and fear grow. But no people are ever an enemy: all peoples have suffered; they all have a good soul! They can all live together!

Religions have a great task: they speak of God to the heart of human beings and liberate them from hatred, prejudice, and fear, opening them up to love. They change men and women from within. Religions can teach every man, every woman, and every people the art of living together through dialogue, mutual esteem, respect of freedom and difference, thus creating a more human world. Because we are all equal, and we are all different.

We need to face our difficulties with a new courage. Turning our eyes far ahead, we must create in dialogue a language made of sympathy, friendship, and compassion. This common language will enable us to talk to each other, beholding the beauty of differences and the value of equality. Living together in peace is God's will. Hatred, division, violence, massacres and genocides do not come from God. Let us ask God in prayer for the gift of peace. Yes, may God grant the world, and us all, the marvelous gift of peace!

Yes, the religious leaders must preach that peace is good and that war is bad; that loving your neighbor is good and that hating your neighbor is bad!

The art of living together and the gift of peace can only come about if we all embrace the common word among us and commit to it through common action in everything we do.

> "Gender and peace are closely linked:
> Peace is vital to promote gender equal-
> ity, while gender inequality can also
> undermine peace and drive conflict and
> violence."

Gender Equality Is Tied to Peace

Hannah Wright

*Hannah Wright is a gender, peace, and security adviser at Safer-
world, an independent security organization. In the following
viewpoint, she suggests that recent conflicts in some developing
countries have hampered progress on the Millennium Development Goals (MDGs). The goals related to women are severely
impacted by conflict and violence, as conflict reduces women's
access to health care and education and often results in limited
economic and political opportunities. Wright reports that it is
also evident that gender inequality can lead to conflict and violence. She says that it is vital that gender equality be a priority
when it comes to formulating a new post-MDGs framework.*

As you read, consider the following questions:

1. According to Wright, how many African countries with the highest maternal mortality ratios in 2008 were experiencing or emerging from serious conflict?

2. What did the United Nations secretary-general recently observe about the Millennium Development Goals (MDGs)?

3. According to the Organisation for Economic Cooperation and Development (OECD), what is crucial to addressing the causes of the conflict in South Sudan?

Progress on the Millennium Development Goals (MDGs) [a set of goals formulated by the United Nations] for women and girls is disappointing, with efforts to improve maternal health among the most off track.

Gender parity in primary school enrollment is close to being achieved, but among the other goals, lack of adequate data makes it difficult to assess whether women and girls are truly benefiting. What is clear is that countries affected by conflict and widespread violence are among the furthest from achieving any of the goals.

As the debate on what to replace the MDGs with after 2015 gathers pace, there are continued calls for gender equality to be central to the framework.

Gender and Peace

Gender and peace are closely linked: Peace is vital to promote gender equality, while gender inequality can also undermine peace and drive conflict and violence. This is one of the key messages in a new briefing, "Gender, Violence and Peace: A Post-2015 Development Agenda," published by Conciliation Resources and Saferworld.

A number of studies have found a strong correlation between levels of conflict and gender inequality, but the nature

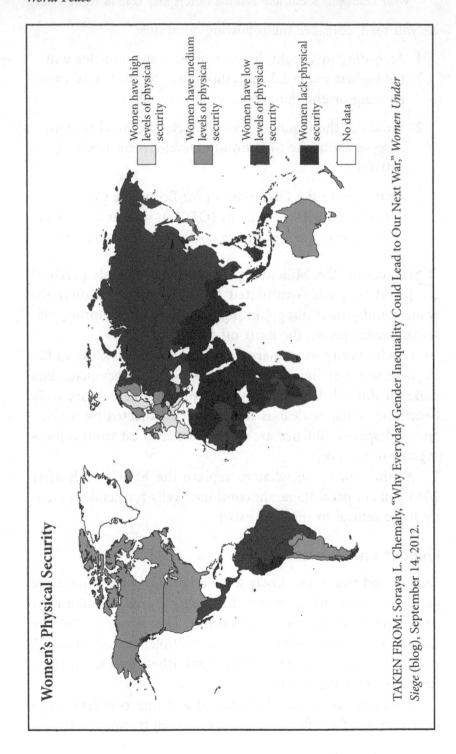

Women's Physical Security

Women have high levels of physical security

Women have medium levels of physical security

Women have low levels of physical security

Women lack physical security

No data

TAKEN FROM: Soraya L. Chemaly, "Why Everyday Gender Inequality Could Lead to Our Next War," *Women Under Siege* (blog), September 14, 2012.

of this relationship is not always clear. Does violence fuel gender inequality, or gender inequality fuel violence, or both? In some cases, women advance their strategic interests during times of conflict, but this is often followed by the restoration of more unequal gender roles afterwards. In many of the countries that have experienced revolutions during the Arab Spring, increased opportunities for women's political activism have been coupled with a violent backlash against women trying to claim their rights.

Conflict and violence have to date been the most important factors obstructing progress on the MDGs. In 2008, the eight African countries with the highest maternal mortality ratios were experiencing or emerging from conflict. As well as causing death, injury and displacement, conflict destroys infrastructure, disrupts markets and social ties, diminishes the capacity of states, and diverts vital resources away from development.

The UN [United Nations] secretary-general, Ban Ki-moon, recently observed that countries experiencing conflict and fragility face most difficulty in achieving the MDGs for women and girls because violence reduces their access to health care and welfare services, economic opportunities and political participation.

Whether gender inequality has an impact on conflict is harder to determine, but there is strong evidence that the gender norms that underpin inequality can drive conflict and violence, particularly when cultural notions of masculinity are associated with domination and control.

South Sudan

Research by Saferworld and others in South Sudan reveals that participation in violent cattle raids, which perpetuates conflict between communities, is seen as a rite of passage for young men. The bride price system, in which cattle are exchanged for girls and women, makes violent cycles of abduction and revenge worse. As a result, the Organisation for Economic Co-operation and Development (OECD) argues that addressing gender norms in South Sudan is crucial to addressing the causes of conflict.

What does all of this mean for discussions about the post-2015 agenda? Those calling for strong commitments on gender equality in the new framework should consider the importance of peace and nonviolence in promoting it. As Saferworld and others have argued, including targets that address the most important drivers of conflict can help to ensure that men and women living in countries vulnerable to violence are not left behind.

The Role of Gender Perspective

Those advocating for peacebuilding commitments in the post-2015 framework would do well to apply a gender perspective to their thinking. A stand-alone goal on gender equality and women's rights can contribute towards peace, particularly if it addresses relevant discriminatory attitudes and social norms. Targets should address the forms of violence that most often affect women as well as men, and commitments on inclusive governance should aim to boost the participation of women and other marginalised groups in decision making. Saferworld's briefing suggests example targets and indicators to these ends.

Next week [in March 2014], UN member states will meet in New York for the annual commission on the status of women, and negotiations have the potential to demonstrate international commitment to making gender equality a key priority for the post-2015 framework. It is vital that member states recognise the importance of overcoming conflict and violence in doing so. Saferworld hopes that those in the women's rights and peacebuilding communities can work together to demonstrate the links between their aims, so the chances of securing strong commitments in both areas are increased.

> "Peace is never achieved through decla-
> rations, through resolutions, through
> slogans. Peace must come through in-
> ner peace."

World Peace Can Only Come Through Inner Peace

The Dalai Lama

The Dalai Lama is the spiritual leader of the Tibetan Buddhist community and a global activist for peace. In the following viewpoint, he reflects on the importance of the twentieth century in world history, noting that although there was tremendous technological and scientific progress, there were also wars, sectarian conflicts, and violence that caused the deaths of two hundred million people. In order to make the twenty-first century a more peaceful era, individuals must focus on finding inner peace. He maintains that religious people, particularly Buddhists, have a responsibility to avoid religious hypocrisy and to be sincere in their practice of their religious and spiritual beliefs—that means eschewing materialism and selfishness, which infect society at large.

As you read, consider the following questions:

1. According to the Dalai Lama, how many Buddhists are there in the world?

2. How old does the Dalai Lama say that Buddha's teachings are?

3. How many volumes of Buddhist thought were translated into Tibetan from Pali, Sanskrit, and Nepalese?

Respected elder Buddhist brothers and sisters, and all others gathered here:

As a Buddhist monk, this is indeed a very moving, very happy moment. As usual, the person who speaks last has nothing to say. All the good points have already been mentioned.

The Importance of Emphasizing the Equality of Everyone as Part of Humanity

My concern or feeling is that of course I'm a Buddhist; but on a further, deeper level, I'm a human being, one of the now nearly seven billion human beings. I'm one of them. Humanity is a social animal, so each individual's future entirely depends on the rest of humanity. So for my own self-interest, I have to think seriously about humanity.

On the fundamental level, on the human level, according to my own experience, I know there are about seven billion human beings. Each one wants a happy life, none of them wants suffering; and each one has every right to achieve that. There's no difference. Whatever religious faith we may be, or as a nonbeliever, or whatever social background we may come from—rich or poor, educated or uneducated, from a royal family or a beggar—we're the same human being on that level. We are the same. We all have the same right.

I think, with many problems that we, humanity as a whole, are facing, we place too much emphasis on the secondary level, the secondary level differences. If we think on a fundamental level that we are all the same human brothers and sisters, then there's no basis to quarrel, no basis to cheat each other, or to look down on each other. We are the same. So we really need to clearly realize that we are the same.

A future happier humanity is everybody's interest, everybody's responsibility. But we Buddhists—I think maybe nearly a thousand million Buddhists—we also have a responsibility to serve humanity. I think Buddha Shakyamuni's motivation for gaining enlightenment was meant for all sentient beings. His whole life and his whole teaching were meant for sentient beings, not only for Buddhists.

Looking Back on the Twentieth Century

Look back at the twentieth century. I think the twentieth century has become a very, very important century in the whole of human history. We invented many, many positive things. And at the same time, the twentieth century has become a century of bloodshed, a century of violence. Even in the name of different religious faiths, there was violence and division. So the twentieth century really has become a century of bloodshed, a century of violence. According to some historians, over two hundred million human beings were killed. If such immense suffering really brought about some good things on this planet, brought a more peaceful, happier world, then such an amount of suffering could be justified. But that's not the case. Even at the beginning of this twenty-first century, there are still some unhealthy things, unhappy things, here and there. These are, I think, the result or symptom of past mistakes, past negligence.

And then also concerning technology, there were immense advances, but that technology also sometimes added to the power of destruction. Science and technology themselves are wonderful; but in order to use them constructively, it ultimately depends on this, our hearts. It depends on the heart of the user of the technology, the user of the science and of the

147

knowledge of science. If you expect a better world to come about from money, to come about from science, to come about from technology, that's wrong. If you really want a better world, a happier world, it ultimately depends on this, our hearts. Intelligence and education are also not very certain to bring about a better world. All these troublemakers we've had—I think, as far as their brains are concerned, these people were very smart. So it's their motivation here in their hearts—anger, fear, hatred, suspicion—they're the cause of these problems.

The Necessity for Inner Peace on an Individual Level

So firstly, in order to make this twenty-first century become a peaceful century, we have to think about inner peace. Peace is never achieved through declarations, through resolutions, through slogans. Peace must come through inner peace. That's the only way. So in order to create a happier world, ultimately you have to look at this, the motivation of each individual. Through a world body like the United Nations, you cannot build peace. Peace must come through people's inner peace, on the individual level.

Avoiding Religious Hypocrisy

Combined individuals—that's society; that's community. But leaders seem to come into society without much concern about moral principles, moral ethics. Society is only concerned about money, power. Then people from that kind of society automatically just think of the importance of money and power. We can't blame these people. Our whole society is thinking this way.

I think many religious people are just paying lip service, saying "God" or "Buddha," but in their actual daily lives, they don't care. We Buddhists pray to Buddha, but in our actual daily lives, we don't care about Buddha—just money, power, fame. What's that? I think we religious people are also sometimes learning hypocrisy. We pray for all sentient beings, but real action? We're not bothered about issues of others' rights. We just exploit. I think many other religious followers also pray, they pray to God—"I believe in God, our creator"—but we creations don't listen to the creator's voice, the creator's guidance.

I often tell my Indian friends that Indian people are comparatively more religious people. They pray to Shiva, Ganesh—I think to Ganesh mainly for wealth. So they're really used to worship, prayer. I think every home has some god statues there. But in their actual lives there's a lot of corruption. How? No god, no Buddha, said corruption is okay. We should be honest and just. No great teacher said, "Oh, you should exploit as much as you can. I will bless you." No god said that.

So therefore if we accept a higher being like Buddha or Jesus Christ or Muhammad or others, then we should be honest people, truthful. Through that way, you yourself also gain more self-confidence: "I have nothing to hide; I can tell anyone what I think and answer anything honestly." Then you get trust from others. So from your own selfish viewpoint, being honest and truthful is a very important source of inner strength, self-confidence. Yes, there are people who speak very nicely and smile, but when you look at their motivation, it's something different. How can you develop trust or respect for them?

Being Sincere in the Practice of Buddhism

I'm Buddhist, and I want to say to my Buddhist brothers and sisters that Buddha's teaching of course is more than two thousand five hundred years old; but still Buddha's teaching is very much relevant in today's world. A number of top scientists are now really eager to get more information and more methods to tackle destructive emotions. The teachings are wonderful, but I really feel now there are signs that there are lamas [spiritual masters] or tulkus [reincarnate lamas] or teachers whose quality has degenerated. This I really feel some concern about. If you yourself don't have a disciplined life, how can you teach that to other people? In order to show others the right path, you yourself must follow the right path.

Now I think all the positive things have already been stated, so now the only thing left is for me to say more negative things. We must be very, very serious. I myself am a Buddhist monk. I always watch myself. Every morning, as soon as I wake up, I remember Buddha and recite some of Buddha's teachings, sort of shaping my mind. Then the rest of my day I should spend according to these principles: being honest, truthful, compassionate, peaceful, nonviolent. So I hope, my Buddhist brothers and sisters here, when you talk about "Buddhadharma [the teachings of the Buddha], Buddhadharma" and promote Buddhadharma, propagate Buddhadharma, first you yourself propagate here in your hearts. So that's something very, very important, one thing—Buddhadharma.

Of course all the other major world religious traditions have the same potential to build inner peace and, through that way, to create a better world. But then one unique thing about Buddhism, Jainism, and part of the Samkhya tradition is the emphasis on the importance of individuals. The ultimate theory or view is that of self-creation. And we believe in the law of causality: If you carry out right actions, positive results come. If you carry out wrong actions, negative things happen. So because of the law of causality, if you do wrong actions, Buddha cannot save you. Buddha taught: "I'll show you the path to go to nirvana [freedom from all suffering], but whether you can achieve that or not is entirely up to you. I cannot lead you through blessings." Buddha never said that.

So you are your own master. That way of teaching I think is very, very helpful. Everything depends on one's own actions.

The Fourteenth Dalai Lama

Tenzin Gyatso, the fourteenth Dalai Lama and leader of the Tibetan Buddhist community, is considered to be one of the most revered and influential spiritual leaders in the world. His lifelong efforts to campaign peacefully on behalf of Tibetan human rights while in exile have inspired human rights and peace activists worldwide. His efforts toward world peace, environmental harmony, and the liberation of oppressed peoples everywhere have made him a symbol of tolerance and respect, as well as a champion of nonviolent resolution to political conflicts. He has also been largely responsible for a growing interest in Tibetan culture and religion in the United States.

"The Fourteenth Dalai Lama,"
Biography in Context. Detroit, MI: Gale, 2014.

Actions, whether positive actions or negative actions, entirely depend on motivation. So Buddhadharma can make, I think, a significant contribution for inner peace like that.

Harmony Among the Different Buddhist Traditions

Now, as I mentioned yesterday [November 29, 2011] when we met the leaders from Burma [also known as Myanmar] and Laos and some others, in the past, because of the names so-called "Hinayana," "Mahayana" and "Tantrayana," people got the impression these three yanas [vehicles] are something really different and separate. That's totally mistaken. As I mentioned briefly this morning, the Theravada tradition, or Pali tradition, is the foundation of Buddhadharma; and the practice of vinaya [monastic vows and discipline] is the foundation of Buddhadharma.

151

Look at Buddha himself, his own story. He cut his own hair and then became a monk. That's the practice of sila [ethical self-discipline]. Then he did six years of meditation. That's the practice of samadhi [absorbed concentration], and also the practice of vipassana [an exceptionally perceptive mind]. Through that way, finally he reached enlightenment. So the three trainings are sila, samadhi, pannya [discriminating awareness, wisdom] or vipassana. So we, his followers, must follow that way. Without the practice of self-discipline, without the practice of vinaya, how can we develop samatha [a stilled and settled mind] and vipassana? Difficult. So the Pali tradition is the foundation of Buddhadharma.

On top of that, comes the practice, I think, of the Prajnaparamita Sutras [The Perfection of Wisdom Sutras], from the Sanskrit tradition, with their emphasis on nirodha [the true stopping of suffering and its causes, true cessation], the third noble truth. So this further explanation is important. What is nirodha? Buddha explained the possibility of eliminating our ignorance. Once we completely eliminate ignorance from our minds, that's nirodha, or moksha [liberation]. So that's a further explanation. And then also magga [the path or understandings for achieving that true stopping, the fourth noble truth] is a further explanation.

So, on the basis of the Pali tradition, then comes the Sanskrit tradition, like the first floor. In other words, first comes the ground floor; that's the Pali tradition—bhikshu [monk] practice, self-discipline, sila. Then comes the first floor, the Prajnaparamita Sutras and also abhidharma [special topics of knowledge], a kind of abhidharma—the teachings about wisdom, the six paramitas [far-reaching attitudes, perfections] or ten paramitas. Then on top of that, the Buddhist Tantrayana—visualization of deities based on practice of vipassana, samatha, and bodhichitta [a mind aimed at attaining enlightenment for the benefit of all]. So these are the ground floor, first floor, and second floor, like that. Without a ground floor, you cannot build the others. So I think the Buddhist brothers and sisters here should know that.

Of course I have no authority. I consider myself a student. Whenever I have time, I always study and read, read, read. As far as Tibetan Buddhism is concerned, about three hundred volumes were translated into Tibetan from Indian languages—Pali, Sanskrit, and some Nepalese. So whenever I have time, I read, think, and study these three hundred volumes. Certainly my knowledge is a little better compared to those people who have never even touched these three hundred volumes. [Based on that knowledge,] as I study these books, I develop the full conviction that the practice of these three trainings is very, very essential.

Becoming Proper Monks

So firstly we Buddhists, whether Theravada or Mahayana or Tantrayana we must be genuine followers of Buddha. That's very important. Clear? In order to become Buddha's followers, we cannot just put on some monk's robe, some bhikshu's robe. We cannot call such people Buddhist monks. We cannot say these are good monks or good bhikshus. Just changing dress is very easy. We need to change here, in our hearts and minds, in order to become a genuine follower of the Buddha. In order to become a Buddhist monk, you must seriously practice self-discipline. Sometimes it looks like: "Oh, let Buddha do all the hard work. We can have a luxurious life." How? How can you? If you're a Buddhist, you must follow Buddha's own way—six years of very hard practice. We must follow his example.

Now, as I mentioned yesterday, a friend spoke about there being some kind of gap or wall between the Pali tradition and the Sanskrit tradition. This wall is to nobody's benefit. We must come together and exchange. There are a lot of things for us to learn from your traditions, from your pratimoksha [monastic vows]. You also can learn some of our Sanskrit pratimoksha. So more regular sort of meetings—not just in a ceremonial way, but serious meetings, serious discussions—are very, very essential. This is one thing.

The Issue of Reviving the Full Nuns' Ordination

Then concerning bhikshunis [fully ordained nuns], as you know, right from the beginning I've supported the revival of bhikshunis in the Mulasarvastivada tradition [that we Tibetans and Mongolians follow]. But we have to follow the vinaya texts. If I had some kind of special right to act like a dictator, then I could say, "Oh, you must do that." That we cannot do. We must follow according to the vinaya texts—the Mulasarvastivada texts and also the Dharmagupta texts [followed in East Asia] and the Theravada texts [followed in Southeast Asia].

You see, this is one important subject we have to discuss very seriously. This decision is beyond my control. What I can decide is to introduce into all the nunneries in the Tibetan community the same level of study that these big monastic institutions can study. And now we already have some nuns becoming geshema [doctors of Buddhist philosophy], good scholars.

From time to time we've discussed the bhikshuni issue and now on this occasion we are doing that as well. I showed the latest letter of appeal to the Laotian Buddhist leader and also to the Burmese Buddhist leader. We will carry on our serious discussion, and I am quite sure eventually we will reach some agreement.

Periodical and Internet Sources Bibliography

The following articles have been selected to supplement the diverse views presented in this chapter.

Lorna Byrne   "Why American Muslim Unity Is So Important to World Peace," *Huffington Post*, March 6, 2014.

Jacob Devaney   "Can Prospect of World War Ignite Global Peace Movement?," *Huffington Post*, September 10, 2013.

John M. Eger   "World Peace Through World Culture," *Huffington Post*, January 1, 2014.

Max Fisher   "Non-Aligned with Reality: How a Global Movement for Peace Became a Club for Tyrants," *Atlantic*, August 29, 2012.

Anne Gearan   "It's Crunchtime for Kerry, and a Middle East Peace Deal," *Washington Post*, January 6, 2014.

Jack Jenkins   "Who Is Leading the Muslim Peace Movement? Millions of Muslims, That's Who," *Think-Progress*, June 18, 2014.

Ann Jones   "Why Peace Is the Business of Men (But Shouldn't Be)," *Mother Jones*, January 13, 2011.

Mia Lombardi   "Would More Female Leadership Lead to Less Global Conflict?," *E-International Relations*, March 28, 2013.

Joseph Nye   "A More Peaceful World If Women in Charge?," CNN, February 8, 2012.

Qasim Rashid   "Muslim Leadership Must Act for World Peace," *Huffington Post*, July 29, 2014.

What Are the Greatest Threats to World Peace?

Chapter Preface

In June 2006, six of the world's most powerful nations agreed to work together to negotiate a diplomatic solution to the problem of Iran's nuclear weapons program. Known as the P5+1, the group consists of the five permanent members of the United Nations Security Council—Russia, China, the United States, France, and the United Kingdom—as well as Germany. The objective of diplomatic talks for the P5+1 countries was an agreement that would effectively constrain the growth of the Iranian nuclear program and bring a halt to the development of nuclear weapons in Iranian facilities. For Iran, the goal was to ease the crippling sanctions that were pummeling the nation's economy and preventing economic growth.

On November 24, 2013, the negotiations resulted in the signing of a historic agreement. Iran agreed to temporarily freeze parts of its nuclear program in exchange for relief on some economic sanctions. Additionally, Iran would allow nuclear inspectors to verify that it was not developing weapons and to monitor aspects of its nuclear energy program. Both sides agreed to further rounds of negotiations to address other outstanding issues.

The reaction to the deal was largely positive. Iranian foreign minister Mohammad Javad Zarif applauded the agreement, pointing out that it would prove that Iran was an honest broker in negotiations and was telling the truth regarding its nuclear ambitions. "It is important that we all of us see the opportunity to end an unnecessary crisis and open new horizons based on respect, based on the rights of the Iranian people and removing any doubts about the exclusively peaceful nature of Iran's nuclear program," he told reporters after the announcement. "This is a process of attempting to restore confidence."

US president Barack Obama also hailed the deal, underscoring the role of diplomacy in reaching a peaceful solution to the Iranian nuclear problem. "Ultimately, only diplomacy can bring about a durable solution to the challenge posed by Iran's nuclear program," he said in his remarks.

However, there was some skepticism about the deal. Some commentators believed that Iran was not going far enough to reduce its nuclear weapons program. Others were concerned about dismantling the sanctions against Iran. Israeli prime minister Benjamin Netanyahu called the deal a "historic mistake" that would not thwart Iran's intent on developing nuclear weapons.

"Today the world has become a much more dangerous place because the most dangerous regime in the world has taken a significant step toward attaining the most dangerous weapon in the world," Netanyahu stated in response to the deal.

Since the November 2013 agreement, there have been several more rounds of talks in efforts to reach a comprehensive deal. A key milestone was reached in May 2014 when the International Atomic Energy Agency (IAEA), an intergovernmental organization tasked with nuclear inspections, verified that Iran was in compliance with the terms of the agreement and was cooperating with its inspectors.

In July 2014, the P5+1 countries and Iran agreed to extend the deadline and keep negotiating aspects of a comprehensive deal on Iran's nuclear program. It is hoped that much of the nation's capability to develop nuclear weapons is dismantled, but that Iran will still be able to produce nuclear energy to meet its growing energy needs.

The risk of a nuclear Iran is discussed in the following chapter, which investigates several threats to world peace. Additional viewpoints examine the threats posed by terrorism, weak American leadership, and global access to clean water.

> "It would be nirvana to live in the world of the Left's imagination—a world in which the U.S. is the greatest threat to peace and stability."

Obama Makes Wars More Likely

Mona Charen

Mona Charen is an author, political commentator, and syndicated columnist. In the following viewpoint, she criticizes President Barack Obama for his weak response to a number of foreign policy challenges, particularly the Syrian civil war and the Ukraine conflict. Charen contends that President Obama's use of soft power and diplomacy has led to the United States losing power and respect around the world and has emboldened tyrants to initiate conflicts and disregard diplomatic agreements. President Obama has also issued empty threats, which have damaged America's reputation abroad. Charen argues that the United States should expect more foreign policy challenges until it is willing to act as a strong global leader once again.

As you read, consider the following questions:

1. According to Charen, in what year did Obama decline to vote for legislation that would have designated Iran's Revolutionary Guard Corps a terrorist organization?

2. How many thousands of Syrian citizens does the viewpoint estimate that the Bashar al-Assad regime has killed?

3. According to the Obama administration, how much of Syria's chemical weapons stockpile had been relinquished by January 2014?

Among the academic set from which President Barack Obama springs, everyone agrees that wars are the result of "arrogance" and bullying by the United States. So concerned was then Sen. Obama about the potential for U.S. aggression that he declined to vote for 2007 legislation that would have designated Iran's Revolutionary Guard Corps [IRGC] as a terrorist organization.

The IRGC had been involved in training and arming terrorists worldwide, particularly in Lebanon (Hezbollah) but also in Afghanistan, Iraq and the Palestinian territories. But Obama worried that such a vote would be "saber rattling."

Our standing in the "world community" (an oxymoron to beat all oxymorons) and our credibility had been badly damaged by just such bellicosity, Obama argued. His administration would deploy "soft power" and diplomacy to make the world safer and more peaceful.

It would be nirvana to live in the world of the Left's imagination—a world in which the U.S. is the greatest threat to peace and stability. Obama has shown greater bellicosity toward Republicans (described as "terrorists with bombs strapped to their chests") than toward our actual adversaries. When Mitt Romney cited Russia a long-term adversary of the

Syria's Civil War

In March of 2011 protesters, inspired by revolts in Egypt and Tunisia, held rallies in the south. Some protesters were shot and killed by security forces. [Bashar al-]Assad responded by firing his cabinet in April. Protests spread across Syria. Snipers fired on crowds, as did tanks sent to restore order. Men were taken into custody, electricity and communication lines were severed, and many fled across the border into Turkey, where they lived in refugee camps. Those who continued to protest called for freedom and democracy, and government forces continued to respond.

According to a United Nations (UN) report, some soldiers who refused to fire on unarmed civilians were executed. As the government continued to try to quell the uprising, President Barack Obama called for Assad's ouster. The United States instituted an investment embargo and the European Union agreed on an oil embargo. NATO [North Atlantic Treaty Organization] took command of air strikes and patrols of the Mediterranean Sea, enforcing a UN arms embargo. In September of 2011 the UN reported nearly 2,700 had been killed as Syrian forces sought to stifle protests against Assad. . . . As of 2013, the violence continued in Syria, and Assad remained in power.

"Bashar al-Assad," Biography in Context.
Detroit, MI: Gale, 2013.

U.S. in 2012, Obama's contempt was glacial: "The '80s called and they want their foreign policy back."

Though the president has repetitively declared that Iran's possession of nuclear weapons would be "unacceptable," his true wish—to accept Iran as a nuclear power in hopes that they will change their behavior—is now unfolding. In Vienna, diplomats from the P5+1 (U.S., U.K., Russia, China, France and Germany) dine on fine cuisine washed down with excellent wines and periodically issued declarations of progress—which usually only means the agreement to meet for more empty discussions. Meanwhile, the severest sanctions against the Iranian regime have been lifted just as they were beginning to bite.

It can't do any harm to talk, right? That was Obama's claim in 2008, when he suggested that he would meet with any rogue leader. He thinks words are like chicken soup—they may not help but they cannot hurt. We're now seeing how dangerous that view is.

First, as Claudia Rosett of *Forbes* writes, the pattern of talks we're engaged in with Iran is identical to what we did with North Korea. "The pattern was one of procedural triumphs . . . followed by Pyongyang's reneging, cheating, pocketing the gains and concessions won at the bargaining table, and walking away."

Formal conclaves that permit evil regimes to gain concessions in exchange for promises they quickly break are one form of dangerous talk. Obama has been perfecting another type as well: the empty threat. "For the sake of the Syrian people, the time has come for President Assad to step aside," the president declared in 2011. Shockingly, the tyrant willing to murder more than 100,000 people and displace millions didn't immediately grab his coat and obey.

Obama did nothing to back his words with actions (like arming the opposition, which was then not dominated by al-Qaida). Later he did something—he spoke more words. This time, it was Obama threatening that well, OK, Bashar [al-] Assad didn't have to go, but if he used chemical weapons, that would cross a "red line for me." (Talk about saber rattling.)

When Assad flamboyantly hopscotched over Obama's red line and received no response, the world rocked on its axis. Though the Obamaites couldn't see it, every small, peace-loving nation in the world was instantly made more vulnerable. Perhaps now, with Russian ships and tanks aiming at Ukraine, they are beginning to understand how international relations work. ("It's not some chessboard," the president asserted recently, displaying his continuing confusion.) No, the game isn't chess; it's more like boxing, where the winner is the stronger one.

The Ukraine crisis flows directly from the Syria debacle, as [Russian president] Vladimir Putin, like Assad, has taken Obama's measure.

The Left heaped scorn on George W. Bush for initially praising Putin, but Bush wised up fast. Obama, by contrast, has submitted passively as Putin put one thumb after another in his eye (Edward Snowden, Assad). Not only has Obama failed to respond vigorously, but he's permitted Putin to play peacemaker in Syria, supposedly presiding over Assad's surrender of chemical weapons. This would be regarded as too risible for fiction, as Russia is Assad's chief sponsor and arms supplier.

In January [2014], the administration, so easily surprised by the world, announced that Syria was "dragging its feet" on removing chemical weapons stockpiles and that only an estimated 4 percent of its supply had been relinquished. "It is the Assad regime's responsibility to transport those chemicals to facilitate removal," said spokesman Jay Carney.

"We expect them to meet their obligation to do so."

Weakness invites aggression. Prepare for more.

> "The ability to ignore unwanted facts is one of the prerogatives of unchallenged power. Closely related is the right to radically revise history."

The Greatest Threat to World Peace

Noam Chomsky

Noam Chomsky is an author, political columnist, and professor of linguistics at the Massachusetts Institute of Technology. In the following viewpoint, he refers to a recent international poll that identified the United States as the greatest threat to peace in the world by a substantial margin. In the Middle East, people overwhelmingly picked the United States and Israel as the biggest threats. Chomsky points out the difference between this international perspective and the view of those in the United States: In American circles, it is Iran that is regarded as a dire threat to world peace. Yet surprisingly, the fact that the United States is considered the greatest threat to world peace by the rest of the world is barely mentioned by American media. Chomsky observes that the US government and a compliant American media have been very adept at either ignoring facts or revising history to fit their own self-interest.

As you read, consider the following questions:

1. According to the WIN/Gallup International poll, what country was voted the second greatest threat to world peace?

2. How many Mexican people does the author report fell into poverty in 2013?

3. Where is the "Wall of Names" located, according to the author?

As the year 2013 drew to an end, the BBC reported on the results of the WIN/Gallup International poll on the question: "Which country do you think is the greatest threat to peace in the world today?"

The United States was the champion by a substantial margin, winning three times the votes of second-place Pakistan.

By contrast, the debate in American scholarly and media circles is about whether Iran can be contained, and whether the huge NSA [National Security Agency] surveillance system is needed to protect U.S. security.

In view of the poll, it would seem that there are more pertinent questions: Can the United States be contained and other nations secured in the face of the U.S. threat?

In some parts of the world, the United States ranks even higher as a perceived menace to world peace, notably in the Middle East, where overwhelming majorities regard the U.S. and its close ally Israel as the major threats they face, not the U.S-Israeli favorite: Iran.

Few Latin Americans are likely to question the judgment of Cuban nationalist hero José Martí, who wrote in 1894, "The further they draw away from the United States, the freer and more prosperous the [Latin] American people will be."

Martí's judgment has been confirmed in recent years, once again by an analysis of poverty by the U.N. [United Nations]

Economic Commission for Latin America and the Caribbean, released last month [in January 2014].

The U.N. report shows that far-reaching reforms have sharply reduced poverty in Brazil, Uruguay, Venezuela and some other countries where U.S. influence is slight, but that it remains abysmal in others—namely, those that have long been under U.S. domination, like Guatemala and Honduras. Even in relatively wealthy Mexico, under the umbrella of the North American Free Trade Agreement, poverty is severe, with 1 million added to the numbers of the poor in 2013.

Sometimes the reasons for the world's concerns are obliquely recognized in the United States, as when former CIA [Central Intelligence Agency] director Michael Hayden, discussing Obama's drone murder campaign, conceded that "right now, there isn't a government on the planet that agrees with our legal rationale for these operations, except for Afghanistan and maybe Israel."

A normal country would be concerned by how it is viewed in the world. Certainly that would be true of a country committed to "a decent respect to the opinions of mankind," to quote the Founding Fathers. But the United States is far from a normal country. It has had the most powerful economy in the world for a century, and has had no real challenge to its global hegemony since World War II, despite some decline, partly self-administered.

The U.S., conscious of "soft power," undertakes major campaigns of "public diplomacy" (aka propaganda) to create a favorable image, sometimes accompanied by worthwhile policies that are welcomed. But when the world persists in believing that the United States is by far the greatest threat to peace, the American press scarcely reports the fact.

The ability to ignore unwanted facts is one of the prerogatives of unchallenged power. Closely related is the right to radically revise history.

A current example can be seen in the laments about the escalating Sunni-Shiite conflict that is tearing apart the Middle East, particularly in Iraq and Syria. The prevailing theme of U.S. commentary is that this strife is a terrible consequence of the withdrawal of American force from the region—a lesson in the dangers of "isolationism."

The opposite is more nearly correct. The roots of the conflict within Islam are many and varied, but it cannot be seriously denied that the split was significantly exacerbated by the American- and British-led invasion of Iraq. And it cannot be too often repeated that aggression was defined at the Nuremberg trials as "the supreme international crime," differing from others in that it encompasses all the evil that follows, including the current catastrophe.

A remarkable illustration of this rapid inversion of history is the American reaction to the current atrocities in Fallujah. The dominant theme is the pain about the sacrifices, in vain, of the American soldiers who fought and died to liberate Fallujah. A look at the news reports of the U.S. assaults on Fallujah in 2004 quickly reveals that these were among the most vicious and disgraceful war crimes of the aggression.

The death of Nelson Mandela provides another occasion for reflection on the remarkable impact of what has been called "historical engineering": reshaping the facts of history to serve the needs of power.

When Mandela at last obtained his freedom, he declared that "during all my years in prison, Cuba was an inspiration and Fidel Castro a tower of strength. . . . [Cuban victories] destroyed the myth of the invincibility of the white oppressor [and] inspired the fighting masses of South Africa . . . a turning point for the liberation of our continent—and of my people—from the scourge of apartheid. . . . What other country can point to a record of greater selflessness than Cuba has displayed in its relations to Africa?"

Nelson Mandela

One of the world's most esteemed and beloved political figures, Nelson Mandela (1918–2013) spent a lifetime fighting for the rights of black South Africans and oppressed people throughout the world. A political prisoner in his native South Africa for nearly 27 years, Mandela became the human embodiment of the struggle against government-mandated discrimination. His courage and determination through decades of imprisonment galvanized not only South African blacks, but also concerned citizens on every continent. After his release from prison in 1990, Mandela reclaimed his leadership role in the once-banned African National Congress (ANC) and fought tirelessly for democratic reform in his troubled homeland. With his magnetic personality and calm demeanor, Mandela was widely regarded as the last best hope for conciliating a peaceful transition to a South African government that would enfranchise all of its citizens, and in a historic election, he won the presidency there in 1994. After his term in office ended in 1999, Mandela . . . continued to work for causes of racial equality, justice, and peace. He established charitable foundations to continue the work that was his life's devotion. . . . He died in 2013 at the age of 95.

"Nelson Mandela," Biography in Context.
Detroit, MI: Gale, 2014.

Today the names of Cubans who died defending Angola from U.S.-backed South African aggression, defying American demands that they leave the country, are inscribed on the "Wall of Names" in Pretoria's Freedom Park. And the thousands of Cuban aid workers who sustained Angola, largely at Cuban expense, are also not forgotten.

The U.S.-approved version is quite different. From the first days after South Africa agreed to withdraw from illegally occupied Namibia in 1988, paving the way for the end of apartheid, the outcome was hailed by the *Wall Street Journal* as a "splendid achievement" of American diplomacy, "one of the most significant foreign policy achievements of the Reagan administration."

The reasons why Mandela and South Africans perceive a radically different picture are spelled out in Piero Gleijeses' masterful scholarly inquiry *Visions of Freedom: Havana, Washington, Pretoria, and the Struggle for Southern Africa, 1976–1991.*

As Gleijeses convincingly demonstrates, South Africa's aggression and terrorism in Angola and its occupation of Namibia were ended by "Cuban military might" accompanied by "fierce black resistance" within South Africa and the courage of Namibian guerrillas. The Namibian liberation forces easily won fair elections as soon as these were possible. Similarly, in elections in Angola, the Cuban-backed government prevailed—while the United States continued to support vicious opposition terrorists there even after South Africa was compelled to back away.

To the end, the Reaganites remained virtually alone in their strong support for the apartheid regime and its murderous depredations in neighboring countries. Though these shameful episodes may be wiped out of internal U.S. history, others are likely to understand Mandela's words.

In these and all too many other cases, supreme power does provide protection against reality—to a point.

*"I want there to be no confusion on this
point: Israel will not allow Iran to get
nuclear weapons. If Israel is forced to
stand alone, Israel will stand alone."*

Iran Is a Threat to World Peace

Benjamin Netanyahu

*Benjamin Netanyahu is the prime minister of Israel. In the fol-
lowing viewpoint, he underscores the dire threat that a nuclear-
armed Iran would pose to the continued existence of Israel, and
he vows that Israel will not allow Iran to develop nuclear weapons. Netanyahu warns the United Nations General Assembly not
to trust the empty promises of Iranian president Hassan Rouhani, warning members that Rouhani has never been a moder-
ate political leader and that he was culpable in earlier attacks on
Americans and Israelis. Netanyahu argues that despite the soothing rhetoric coming from Rouhani, it is clear that Iran is developing nuclear weapons. The international community must not
be fooled and must continue to apply tough sanctions on Iran
along with a credible military threat if Iran does not back down.*

Benjamin Netanyahu, "Remarks of Benjamin Netanyahu to the United Nations General
Assembly," Israel Ministry of Foreign Affairs, October 1, 2013. Reproduced by permission.

As you read, consider the following questions:

1. According to Netanyahu, how many years ago did King Cyrus end the Babylonian exile of the Jewish people?

2. According to the viewpoint, what year was Iran caught red-handed secretly building an underground centrifuge facility at Natanz?

3. What facility does Netanyahu identify as indispensable to Iran's nuclear weapons program?

I feel deeply honored and privileged to stand here before you today [in October 2013] representing the citizens of the State of Israel. We are an ancient people. We date back nearly 4,000 years to Abraham, Isaac and Jacob. We have journeyed through time. We've overcome the greatest of adversities.

And we reestablished our sovereign state in our ancestral homeland, the land of Israel.

The Jewish people's odyssey through time has taught us two things. Never give up hope, always remain vigilant. Hope charts the future. Vigilance protects it.

The Threat of Iran

Today, our hope for the future is challenged by a nuclear-armed Iran that seeks our destruction. But I want you to know, that wasn't always the case. Some 2500 years ago, the great Persian King Cyrus ended the Babylonian exile of the Jewish people. He issued a famous edict in which he proclaimed the right of the Jews to return to the Land of Israel and rebuild the Jewish Temple in Jerusalem. That's a Persian decree, and thus began a historic friendship between the Jews and the Persian that lasted until modern times.

But in 1979, a radical regime in Tehran tried to stamp out that friendship. As it was busy crushing the Iranian people's hopes for democracy, it also led wild chants of "Death to the Jews!" Now, since that time, presidents of Iran have come and gone. Some presidents were considered moderates, others hard-liners. But they've all served that same unforgiving creed, that same unforgetting regime—that creed that is espoused and enforced by the real power in Iran, the dictator known in Iran as the Supreme Leader, first Ayatollah [Ruhollah] Khomeini and now Ayatollah [Ali] Khamenei. President [Hassan] Rouhani, like the presidents who came before him, is a loyal servant of the regime. He was one of only six candidates the regime permitted to run for office. Nearly 700 other candidates were rejected.

Rouhani's Credentials

So what made him acceptable? Well, Rouhani headed Iran's Supreme National Security Council from 1989 through 2003. During that time, Iran's henchmen gunned down opposition leaders in a Berlin restaurant. They murdered 85 people at the Jewish Community Center in Buenos Aires. They killed 19 American soldiers by blowing up the Khobar Towers in Saudi Arabia.

Are we to believe that Rouhani, the National Security Advisor of Iran at the time, knew nothing about these attacks?

Of course he did.

Just as 30 years ago, Iran's security chiefs knew about the bombings in Beirut that killed 241 American marines and 58 French paratroopers.

Rouhani was also Iran's chief nuclear negotiator between 2003 and 2005. He masterminded the strategy which enabled Iran to advance its nuclear weapons program behind a smoke-screen of diplomatic engagement and very soothing rhetoric. Now I know Rouhani does not sound like [former Iranian president Mahmoud] Ahmadinejad. But when it comes to Iran's nuclear weapons program, the only difference between them is this: Ahmadinejad was a wolf in wolf's clothing and

Rouhani is a wolf in sheep's clothing—a wolf who thinks he can pull the wool over the eyes of the international community.

Like everyone else, I wish we could believe Rouhani's words. But we must focus on Iran's actions.

And it's the brazen contrast, this extraordinary contradiction between Rouhani's words and Iran's actions that is so startling. Rouhani stood at this very podium last week and praised Iranian democracy. Iranian democracy, he said.

Iran's Hypocrisy

But the regime that he represents executes political dissidents by the hundreds and jails them by the thousands. Rouhani spoke of "the human tragedy in Syria." Yet Iran directly participates in [Bashar al-]Assad's murder and massacre of tens of thousands of innocent men, women, and children in Syria, and that regime is propping up a Syrian regime that just used chemical weapons against its own people.

Rouhani condemned the "violent scourge of terrorism." Yet in the last three years alone Iran has ordered, planned or perpetrated terrorist attacks in 25 cities on five continents.

Rouhani denounces "attempts to change the regional balance through proxies." Yet Iran is actively destabilizing Lebanon, Yemen, Bahrain, and many other Middle Eastern countries.

Rouhani promises "constructive engagement with other countries." Yet two years ago, Iranian agents tried to assassinate Saudi Arabia's ambassador in Washington, DC.

And just three weeks ago, an Iranian agent was arrested trying to collect information for possible attacks against the American embassy in Tel Aviv. Some constructive engagement!

I wish I could be moved by Rouhani's invitation to join his "WAVE"—the World Against Violence and Extremism. Yet the only waves Iran has generated in the last 30 years are waves of violence and terrorism that it has unleashed on the region and across the world. . . .

I wish I could believe Rouhani, but I don't because facts are stubborn things. And the facts are that Iran's savage record flatly contradicts Rouhani's soothing rhetoric.

Iran's Nuclear Program

Last Friday, Rouhani assured us that in pursuit of its nuclear program, Iran has "never chosen deceit . . . and secrecy." Never chosen deceit and secrecy?!

Well, in 2002, Iran was caught red-handed secretly building an underground centrifuge facility at Natanz. Then in 2009, Iran was again caught red-handed secretly building a huge underground nuclear facility for uranium enrichment in a mountain near Qom. Rouhani tells us not to worry: He assures us that all this is not intended for nuclear weapons. Do any of you believe that? If you believe that, here's a few questions that you might want to ask:

Why would a country that claims to only want peaceful nuclear energy, why would such a country build hidden underground enrichment facilities?

Why would a country with vast natural energy reserves invest billions in developing nuclear energy?

Why would a country intent on merely civilian nuclear programs continue to defy multiple Security Council resolutions and incur the costs of crippling sanctions on its economy?

And why would a country with a peaceful nuclear program develop intercontinental ballistic missiles [ICBMs] whose sole purpose is to deliver nuclear warheads? You don't build ICBMs to carry TNT thousands of miles away. You build them for one purpose—to carry nuclear warheads. And Iran is now building ICBMs that the United States says can reach this city in three or four years.

Why would they do all this? The answer is simple. Iran is not building a peaceful nuclear program. Iran is developing nuclear weapons.

Last year alone, Iran enriched three tons of uranium to 3.5%, doubled its stockpile of 20% enriched uranium, and added thousands of new centrifuges, including advanced centrifuges. It also continued work on the heavy water reactor in Arak. That's in order to have another route to the bomb—a plutonium path.

And since Rouhani's election—and I stress this—this vast and feverish effort has continued unabated. . . .

Underground nuclear facilities? Heavy water reactors? Advanced centrifuges? ICBMs?

Analyzing the Evidence

It's not that it's hard to find evidence that Iran has a nuclear weapons program. It's hard to find evidence that Iran doesn't have a nuclear weapons program.

Last year when I spoke here at the UN [United Nations], I drew a red line. Iran has been very careful not to cross that line. But Iran is positioning itself to race across that line in the future at a time of its choosing. Iran wants to be in a position to rush forward to build nuclear bombs before the international community can detect it, much less prevent it.

Yet Iran faces one big problem, and that problem is summed up in one word: Sanctions.

Imposing Tough Sanctions

I have argued for many years, including on this podium, that the only way to peacefully prevent Iran from developing nuclear weapons is to combine tough sanctions with a credible military threat. And that policy is today bearing fruit. Thanks to the efforts of many countries, many represented here, and under the leadership of the United States, tough sanctions have taken a big bite out of Iran's economy. Oil revenues have fallen. The currency has plummeted. Banks are hard-pressed to transfer money.

So as a result, the regime is under intense pressure from the Iranian people to get the sanctions removed. That's why Rouhani got elected in the first place. That's why he launched his charm offensive.

He definitely wants to get the sanctions lifted, I guarantee you that, but he doesn't want to give up Iran's nuclear weapons program in return.

Rouhani's Strategy

Now, here's the strategy to achieve this.

First, smile a lot. Smiling never hurts. Second, pay lip service to peace, democracy and tolerance. Third, offer meaningless concessions in exchange for lifting sanctions. And fourth, and the most important, ensure that Iran retains sufficient nuclear material and sufficient nuclear infrastructure to race to the bomb at a time that it chooses to do so. You know why Rouhani thinks he can get away with this? I mean, this is a ruse; it's a ploy. Why does Rouhani think he can get away with it? Because he's gotten away with it before. Because his strategy of talking a lot and doing little has worked for him in the past. He even bragged about it. Here's what he said in his 2011 book about his time as Iran's chief nuclear negotiator: "While we were talking to the Europeans in Tehran, we were installing equipment in Isfahan. . . ."

For those of you who don't know, the Isfahan facility is an indispensable part of Iran's nuclear weapons program. That's where uranium ore called yellowcake is converted into an enrichable form. Rouhani boasted, and I quote: "By creating a calm environment, we were able to complete the work in Isfahan."

He fooled the world once. Now he thinks he can fool it again. You see, Rouhani thinks he can have his yellowcake and eat it too.

The Case of North Korea

And he has another reason to believe that he can get away with this, and that reason is called North Korea.

Like Iran, North Korea also said its nuclear program was for peaceful purposes. Like Iran, North Korea also offered meaningless concessions and empty promises in return for sanctions relief. In 2005, North Korea agreed to a deal that was celebrated the world over by many well-meaning people. Here is what a *New York Times* editorial had to say about it: "For years now, foreign policy insiders have pointed to North Korea as the ultimate nightmare ... a closed, hostile and paranoid dictatorship with an aggressive nuclear weapons program.

"Very few could envision a successful outcome.

"And yet North Korea agreed in principle this week to dismantle its nuclear weapons program, return to the NPT [nuclear power treaty], abide by the treaty's safeguards and admit international inspectors. ...

"Diplomacy, it seems, does work after all."

End quote. ...

A year later, North Korea exploded its first nuclear weapons device.

Yet as dangerous as a nuclear-armed North Korea is, it pales in comparison to the danger of a nuclear-armed Iran. A nuclear-armed Iran would have a chokehold on the world's main energy supplies. It would trigger nuclear proliferation throughout the Middle East, turning the most unstable part of the planet into a nuclear tinderbox. And for the first time in history, it would make the specter of nuclear terrorism a clear and present danger.

A nuclear-armed Iran in the Middle East wouldn't be another North Korea. It would be another 50 North Koreas!

The Lessons of History

I know that some in the international community think I'm exaggerating this threat. Sure, they know that Iran's regime leads these chants, "Death to America!," "Death to Israel!," then it pledges to wipe Israel off the map. But they think this wild rhetoric is just bluster for domestic consumption. Have these people learned nothing from history?

The last century has taught us that when a radical regime with global ambitions gets awesome power, sooner or later, its appetite for aggression knows no bounds. That's the central lesson of the 20th century. Now, we cannot forget it.

The world may have forgotten this lesson. The Jewish people have not.

Iran's fanaticism is not bluster. It's real. This fanatic regime must never be allowed to arm itself with nuclear weapons.

I know that the world is weary of war. We in Israel, we know all too well the cost of war. But history has taught us that to prevent war tomorrow, we must be firm today.

Confronting the Threat

This raises the question: Can diplomacy stop this threat?

Well, the only diplomatic solution that would work is one that fully dismantles Iran's nuclear weapons program and prevents it from having one in the future. President [Barack] Obama rightly said that Iran's conciliatory words must be matched by transparent, verifiable and meaningful action, and to be meaningful, a diplomatic solution would require Iran to do four things. First, cease all uranium enrichment. This is called for by several Security Council resolutions. Second, remove from its territory the stockpiles of enriched uranium. Third, dismantle the infrastructure for a nuclear breakout capability, including the underground facility near Qom and the advanced centrifuges in Natanz. And four, stop all work at the heavy water reactor in Arak aimed at the production of plutonium.

Israel and Iran's Nuclear Program

Israel views the possibility of an Iranian nuclear weapon as a threat to its existence due to repeated warnings by Iran that it would destroy Israel. Although Israel does not confirm its status as a nuclear power, it does not deny that it has nuclear weapons. Israel has pledged repeatedly to take whatever military action it deems appropriate to ensure its security and has mounted conventional weapons attacks against suspected nuclear facilities in Iraq and Syria in the past. Because Iran has openly denied Israel's right to exist and has repeatedly threatened to annihilate the country, Israeli officials indicated that their patience with Iran regarding openness about its nuclear program was limited.

"Iran Nuclear Program,"
Global Issues in Context Online Collection.
Detroit, MI: Gale, 2014.

These steps would put an end to Iran's nuclear weapons program and eliminate its breakout capability. There are those who would readily agree to leave Iran with a residual capability to enrich uranium. I advise them to pay close attention to what Rouhani said in a speech to Iran's Supreme Cultural Revolution Council. This was published in 2005: "A country that can enrich uranium to about 3.5% will also have the capability to enrich it to about 90%. Having fuel cycle capability virtually means that a country that possesses this capability is able to produce nuclear weapons."

Precisely. This is precisely why Iran's nuclear weapons program must be fully and verifiably dismantled. And this is why the pressure on Iran must continue.

So here's what the international community must do. First, keep up the sanctions. If Iran advances its nuclear weapons program during negotiations, strengthen the sanctions.

Second, don't agree to a partial deal. A partial deal would lift international sanctions that have taken years to put in place in exchange for cosmetic concessions that will take only weeks for Iran to reverse. Third, lift the sanctions only when Iran fully dismantles its nuclear weapons program. . . .

Applying Pressure

The international community has Iran on the ropes. If you want to knock out Iran's nuclear weapons program peacefully, don't let up the pressure. Keep it up.

We all want to give diplomacy with Iran a chance to succeed. But when it comes to Iran, the greater the pressure, the greater the chance.

Three decades ago, President Ronald Reagan famously advised: Trust but verify. When it comes to Iran's nuclear weapons program, here's my advice: Distrust, Dismantle, and Verify. . . .

Israel will never acquiesce to nuclear arms in the hands of a rogue regime that repeatedly promises to wipe us off the map. Against such a threat, Israel will have no choice but to defend itself. I want there to be no confusion on this point: Israel will not allow Iran to get nuclear weapons. If Israel is forced to stand alone, Israel will stand alone. Yet in standing alone, Israel will know that we will be defending many, many others. The dangers of a nuclear-armed Iran and the emergence of other threats in our region have led many of our Arab neighbors to finally recognize that Israel is not their enemy. This affords us the opportunity to overcome historic animosities and build new relationships, new friendships, new hopes. Israel welcomes engagement with the wider Arab world. We hope that our common interests and common challenges will help us forge a more peaceful future.

Israeli-Palestinian Relations

And Israel continues to seek a historic peace with our Palestinian neighbors, one that ends our conflict once and for all. We want a peace based on security and mutual recognition in which a demilitarized Palestinian state recognizes the Jewish state of Israel. I remain committed to achieving a historic conciliation and building a better future for Israelis and Palestinians alike.

Now, I have no illusions about how difficult this will be to achieve. Twenty years ago, the peace process between Israel and the Palestinians began. Six Israeli prime ministers, myself included, have not succeeded in achieving peace with the Palestinians. My predecessors were prepared to make painful concessions. So am I.

But so far, Palestinian leaders haven't been prepared to offer the painful concessions they must make to end the conflict. For peace to be achieved, the Palestinians must finally recognize the Jewish state and Israel's security needs must be met. I am prepared to make a historic compromise for a genuine and enduring peace. But I will never compromise on the security of my people and of my country of the one and only Jewish state. . . .

Keeping a Promise

One cold day in the late 19th century, my grandfather Nathan and his younger brother Judah were standing in a railway station in the heart of Europe. They were seen by a group of anti-Semitic hoodlums who ran towards them waving clubs, screaming, "Death to the Jews!"

My grandfather shouted to his younger brother to flee and save himself. And he then stood alone against the raging mob to slow it down. They beat him senseless. They left him for dead. Before he passed out, covered in his own blood, he said to himself: "What a disgrace! What a disgrace! The descendants of the Maccabees lie in the mud, powerless to defend themselves."

He promised himself then that if he lived, he would take his family to the Jewish homeland to help build a future for the Jewish people. I stand here today as Israel's prime minister because my grandfather kept that promise.

So many other Israelis have a similar story: a parent or a grandparent who fled every conceivable oppression, and came to Israel to start a new life in our ancient homeland.

Together, we've transformed a bludgeoned Jewish people left for dead into a vibrant, thriving nation, defending itself with the courage of modern Maccabees, developing limitless possibilities for the future.

In our time the biblical prophecies are being realized. As the prophet Amos said,

They shall rebuild ruined cities and inhabit them.

They shall plant vineyards and drink their wine.

They shall till gardens and eat their fruit.

And I will plant them upon their soil never to be uprooted again.

> *"Iran poses absolutely no threat to the world or the region. In fact, in ideals as well as in actual practice, my country has been a harbinger of just peace and comprehensive security."*

Iran Is Not a Threat to World Peace

Hassan Rouhani

Hassan Rouhani is the seventh president of Iran. In the following viewpoint, he rejects the prevalent opinion in the West that Iran is a serious threat to world peace, accusing some nations of demonizing Iran and other Middle Eastern countries. He declares that Iran's nuclear program is pursuing exclusively peaceful purposes and that nuclear weapons have no place in Iran's security policy. However, he insists that Iran has a right to develop a nuclear program for its energy needs and will continue to do so. He argues that imposing unjust sanctions are essentially inhumane to the Iranian people and should be lifted out of a concern for human suffering. He suggests that Iranian authorities are willing to engage in talks to provide verification of the state of Iran's nuclear program. Rouhani proposes a new group, WAVE, the World Against Violence and Extremism, to support world peace and eliminate war, injustice, poverty, and oppression.

Hassan Rouhani, "Remarks of Iranian President Hassan Rouhani to the United Nations General Assembly," www.un.org, September 24, 2013. Reproduced by permission.

As you read, consider the following questions:

1. What nation does Rouhani say is under occupation and suffering under an apartheid rule?

2. According to Rouhani, what atrocity happened to some Iranian nuclear scientists?

3. What movement does Rouhani urge members to consider instead of the "Coalitions for War" in various parts of the world?

Mr. President, Mr. Secretary-General, Excellencies, Ladies and Gentlemen,

At the outset, I would like to offer my most sincere felicitations on your deserved election to the presidency of the General Assembly and seize the moment to express appreciation for the valuable efforts of our distinguished secretary-general.

Our world today is replete with fear and hope; fear of war and hostile regional and global relations; fear of deadly confrontation of religious, ethnic and national identities; fear of institutionalization of violence and extremism; fear of poverty and destructive discrimination; fear of decay and destruction of life-sustaining resources; fear of disregard for human dignity and rights; and fear of neglect of morality. Alongside these fears, however, there are new hopes; the hope of universal acceptance by the people and the elite all across the globe of "yes to peace and no to war"; and the hope of preference of dialogue over conflict, and moderation over extremism.

The recent elections in Iran represent a clear, living example of the wise choice of hope, rationality and moderation by the great people of Iran. The realization of democracy consistent with religion and the peaceful transfer of executive power manifested that Iran is the anchor of stability in an otherwise ocean of regional instabilities. The firm belief of our people and government in enduring peace, stability, tranquility, peaceful resolution of disputes and reliance on the ballot box as the basis of power, public acceptance and legitimacy has indeed played a key role in creating such a safe environment.

Mr. President, Ladies and Gentlemen,

The current critical period of transition in international relations is replete with dangers, albeit with unique opportunities. Any miscalculation of one's position, and of course, of others, will bear historic damages; a mistake by one actor will have a negative impact on all others. Vulnerability is now a global and indivisible phenomenon.

At this sensitive juncture in the history of global relations, the age of zero-sum games is over, even though a few actors still tend to rely on archaic and deeply ineffective ways and means to preserve their old superiority and domination. Militarism and the recourse to violent and military means to subjugate others are failed examples of the perpetuation of old ways in new circumstances.

Coercive economic and military policies and practices geared to the maintenance and preservation of old superiorities and dominations have been pursued in a conceptual mindset that negates peace, security, human dignity, and exalted human ideals. Ignoring differences between societies and globalizing Western values as universal ones represent another manifestation of this conceptual mind-set. Yet another reflection of the same cognitive model is the persistence of Cold War mentality and bipolar division of the world into "superior us" and "inferior others." Fanning fear and phobia around the emergence of new actors on the world scene is another.

In such an environment, governmental and nongovernmental, religious, ethnic, and even racial violence has increased, and there is no guarantee that the era of quiet among big powers will remain immune from such violent discourses, practices and actions. The catastrophic impact of violent and extremist narratives should not—in fact, must not—be underestimated.

In this context, the strategic violence, which is manifested in the efforts to deprive regional players from their natural domain of action, containment policies, regime change from outside, and the efforts towards redrawing of political borders and frontiers, is extremely dangerous and provocative.

The prevalent international political discourse depicts a civilized center surrounded by uncivilized peripheries. In this picture, the relation between the center of world power and the peripheries is hegemonic. The discourse assigning the north the center stage and relegating the south to the periphery has led to the establishment of a monologue at the level of international relations. The creation of illusory identity distinctions and the current prevalent violent forms of xenophobia are the inevitable outcome of such a discourse. Propagandistic and unfounded faith-phobic, Islamo-phobic, Shia-phobic, and Iran-phobic discourses do indeed represent serious threats against world peace and human security.

This propagandistic discourse has assumed dangerous proportions through portrayal and inculcation of presumed imaginary threats. One such imaginary threat is the so-called "Iranian threat"—which has been employed as an excuse to justify a long catalogue of crimes and catastrophic practices over the past three decades. The arming of the Saddam Hussein regime with chemical weapons and supporting the Taliban and al-Qaida are just two examples of such catastrophes. Let me say this in all sincerity before this august world assembly, that based on irrefutable evidence, those who harp on the so-called threat of Iran are either a threat against international peace and security themselves or promote such a threat. Iran poses absolutely no threat to the world or the region. In fact, in ideals as well as in actual practice, my country has been a harbinger of just peace and comprehensive security.

Mr. President, Ladies and Gentlemen,

Nowhere in the world has violence been so deadly and destructive as in North Africa and West Asia. Military intervention in Afghanistan, Saddam Hussein's imposed war against Iran, occupation of Kuwait, military interventions against Iraq, brutal repression of the Palestinian people, assassination of common people and political figures in Iran, and terrorist bombings in countries such as Iraq, Afghanistan and Lebanon are examples of violence in this region in the last three decades.

What has been—and continues to be—practiced against the innocent people of Palestine is nothing less than structural violence. Palestine is under occupation; the basic rights of the Palestinians are tragically violated, and they are deprived of the right of return and access to their homes, birthplace and homeland. Apartheid as a concept can hardly describe the crimes and the institutionalized aggression against the innocent Palestinian people.

The human tragedy in Syria represents a painful example of the catastrophic spread of violence and extremism in our region. From the very outset of the crisis and when some regional and international actors helped to militarize the situation through infusion of arms and intelligence into the country and active support of extremist groups, we emphasized that there was no military solution to the Syrian crisis. Pursuit of expansionist strategies and objectives and attempts to change the regional balance through proxies cannot be camouflaged behind humanitarian rhetoric. The common objective of the international community should be a quick end to the killing of the innocent. While condemning any use of chemical weapons, we welcome Syria's acceptance of the Chemical Weapons Convention, and believe that the access by extremist terrorist groups to such weapons is the greatest danger to the region that must be considered in any disarmament plan. Simultaneously, I should underline that illegitimate and ineffective threats to use or the actual use of force will only lead to further exacerbation of violence and crisis in the region.

Terrorism and the killing of innocent people represent the ultimate inhumanity of extremism and violence. Terrorism is a violent scourge and knows no country or national borders. But, the violence and extreme actions such as the use of drones against innocent people in the name of combating terrorism should also be condemned. Here, I should also say a word about the criminal assassination of Iranian nuclear scientists. For what crimes have they been assassinated? The United Nations and the Security Council should answer the question: Have the perpetrators been condemned?

Unjust sanctions, as manifestation of structural violence, are intrinsically inhumane and against peace. And contrary to the claims of those who pursue and impose them, it is not the states and the political elite that are targeted, but rather, it is the common people who are victimized by these sanctions. Let us not forget millions of Iraqis who, as a result of sanctions covered in international legal jargon, suffered and lost their lives, and many more who continue to suffer all through their lives. These sanctions are violent, pure and simple; whether called smart or otherwise, unilateral or multilateral. These sanctions violate inalienable human rights, inter alia, the right to peace, right to development, right to access to health and education, and above all, the right to life. Sanctions, beyond any and all rhetoric, cause belligerence, war-mongering and human suffering. It should be borne in mind, however, that the negative impact is not merely limited to the intended victims of sanctions; it also affects the economy and livelihood of other countries and societies, including the countries imposing sanctions.

Mr. President, Excellencies,

Violence and extremism nowadays have gone beyond the physical realm and have unfortunately afflicted and tarnished

A New Era?

In September 2013, newly elected Iranian president Hassan Rouhani (1948–) struck a different tone from his predecessor, [Mahmoud] Ahmadinejad, over Iran's nuclear program. After releasing eleven political prisoners, Rouhani told a U.S. news broadcaster that Iran would never build nuclear weapons. Rouhani also stressed that he had power to negotiate with the West over Iran's uranium enrichment program, indicating that [Ayatollah Ali] Khamenei had given his blessing to Rouhani on the issue. In a speech before the United Nations delivered on 24 September, Rouhani reiterated his desire for Iran to seek a civilian nuclear program without developing nuclear weapons. Rouhani later called for an agreement on the Iranian nuclear issue within a matter of months. The United States and Iran announced that U.S. secretary of state John Kerry (1943–) and Iranian foreign minister Mohammad Javad Zarif (1960–) would work together on the issue, marking the first meeting in years between high-ranking government officials from the two nations.

"Iran Nuclear Program,"
Global Issues in Context Online Collection.
Detroit, MI: Gale, 2014.

the mental and spiritual dimensions of life in human societies. Violence and extremism leave no space for understanding and moderation as the necessary foundations of collective life of human beings and the modern society. Intolerance is the predicament of our time. We need to promote and reinforce tolerance in light of the religious teachings and appropriate cultural and political approaches. The human society should be elevated from a state of mere tolerance to that of collective collaboration. We should not just tolerate others. We should rise above mere tolerance and dare to work together.

People all over the world are tired of war, violence and extremism. They hope for a change in the status quo. And this is a unique opportunity—for us all. The Islamic Republic of Iran believes that all challenges can be managed—successfully—through a smart, judicious blend of hope and moderation. Warmongers are bent on extinguishing all hope. But hope for change for the better is an innate, religious, widespread, and universal concept.

Hope is founded on the belief in the universal will of the people across the globe to combat violence and extremism, to cherish change, to oppose imposed structures, to value choice, and to act in accordance with human responsibility. Hope is no doubt one of the greatest gifts bestowed upon human beings by their all-loving creator. And moderation is to think and move in a wise, judicious manner, conscious of the time and the space, and to align exalted ideals with choice of effective strategies and policies, while cognizant of objective realities.

The Iranian people, in a judiciously sober choice in the recent elections, voted for the discourse of hope, foresight and prudent moderation—both at home and abroad. In foreign policy, the combination of these elements means that the Islamic Republic of Iran, as a regional power, will act responsibly with regard to regional and international security, and is willing and prepared to cooperate in these fields, bilaterally as well as multilaterally, with other responsible actors. We defend peace based on democracy and the ballot box everywhere, including in Syria, Bahrain, and other countries in the region, and believe that there are no violent solutions to world crises. The bitter and ugly realities of the human society can only be overcome through recourse to and reliance on human wisdom, interaction and moderation. Securing peace and democracy and ensuring the legitimate rights of all countries in the world, including in the Middle East, cannot—and will not—be realized through militarism.

Iran seeks to resolve problems, not to create them. There is no issue or dossier that cannot be resolved through reliance on hope and prudent moderation, mutual respect, and rejection of violence and extremism. Iran's nuclear dossier is a case in point. As clearly stated by the leader of the Islamic Revolution, acceptance of the inalienable right of Iran constitutes the best and the easiest way of resolving this issue. This is not political rhetoric. Rather, it is based on a profound recognition of the state of technology in Iran, global political environment, the end of the era of zero-sum games, and the imperative of seeking common objectives and interests towards reaching common understanding and shared security. Put otherwise, Iran and other actors should pursue two common objectives as two mutually inseparable parts of a political solution for the nuclear dossier of Iran.

1. Iran's nuclear program—and for that matter, that of all other countries—must pursue exclusively peaceful purposes. I declare here, openly and unambiguously, that, notwithstanding the positions of others, this has been, and will always be, the objective of the Islamic Republic of Iran. Nuclear weapons and other weapons of mass destruction have no place in Iran's security and defense doctrine, and contradict our fundamental religious and ethical convictions. Our national interests make it imperative that we remove any and all reasonable concerns about Iran's peaceful nuclear program.

2. The second objective, that is, acceptance of and respect for the implementation of the right to enrichment inside Iran and enjoyment of other related nuclear rights, provides the only path towards achieving the first objective. Nuclear knowledge in Iran has been domesticated now and the nuclear technology, inclusive of enrichment, has already

reached industrial scale. It is, therefore, an illusion, and extremely unrealistic, to presume that the peaceful nature of the nuclear program of Iran could be ensured through impeding the program via illegitimate pressures.

In this context, the Islamic Republic of Iran, insisting on the implementation of its rights and the imperative of international respect and cooperation in this exercise, is prepared to engage immediately in time-bound and result-oriented talks to build mutual confidence and removal of mutual uncertainties with full transparency.

Iran seeks constructive engagement with other countries based on mutual respect and common interest, and within the same framework does not seek to increase tensions with the United States. I listened carefully to the statement made by President Obama today at the General Assembly. Commensurate with the political will of the leadership in the United States and hoping that they will refrain from following the shortsighted interest of warmongering pressure groups, we can arrive at a framework to manage our differences. To this end, equal footing, mutual respect, and the recognized principles of international law should govern the interactions. Of course, we expect to hear a consistent voice from Washington.

Mr. President, Ladies and Gentlemen,

In recent years, a dominant voice has been repeatedly heard: "The military option is on the table." Against the backdrop of this illegal and ineffective contention, let me say loud and clear that "peace is within reach." So, in the name of the Islamic Republic of Iran I propose, as a starting step, the consideration by the United Nations of the project: "the World Against Violence and Extremism" (WAVE). Let us all join this "WAVE." I invite all states, international organizations and civil institutions to undertake a new effort to guide the world in this direction. We should start thinking about "Coalition for Enduring Peace" all across the globe instead of the ineffective "Coalitions for War" in various parts of the world.

Today, the Islamic Republic of Iran invites you and the entire world community to take a step forward; an invitation to join the WAVE: World Against Violence and Extremism. We should accept and be able to open a new horizon in which peace will prevail over war, tolerance over violence, progress over bloodletting, justice over discrimination, prosperity over poverty, and freedom over despotism. As beautifully said by Ferdowsi, the renowned Iranian epic poet:

Be relentless in striving for the cause of Good.

Bring the spring, you must, Banish the winter, you should.

Notwithstanding all difficulties and challenges, I am deeply optimistic about the future. I have no doubt that the future will be bright with the entire world solidly rejecting violence and extremism. Prudent moderation will ensure a bright future for the world. My hope, aside from personal and national experience, emanates from the belief shared by all divine religions that a good and bright future awaits the world. As stated in the Holy Qur'an:

And We proclaimed in the Psalms, after We had proclaimed in the Torah, that My virtuous servants will inherit the earth. (21:105)

Thank you, Mr. President.

> "Counterterrorism remains our top priority. The FBI works with our law enforcement and intelligence community (IC) partners to integrate intelligence and operations and to detect and disrupt terrorists and their organizations."

Terrorism Is a Threat to World Peace

James B. Comey

James B. Comey is the director of the Federal Bureau of Investigation (FBI). In the following viewpoint, he maintains that terrorism continues to be a serious threat to world peace and the security of the United States. He says that America faces a range of terrorist threats, including those from foreign terrorist organizations, homegrown radicals, cyberterrorists, and active shooters. He explains that groups known for operating within a certain African or Middle Eastern country can develop the capability of carrying out attacks on neighboring regions and even strike the West. Such threats must be met with proactive law enforcement and intelligence groups that have the resources to identify and monitor potential terrorists, investigate leads, and develop cases.

James B. Comey, "Statement before the Senate Committee on Homeland Security and Governmental Affairs," www.fbi.gov, November 14, 2013.

Comey concludes that the FBI has prioritized counterterrorism in the United States and will continue to protect the nation from all terroristic threats.

As you read, consider the following questions:

1. According to Comey, when did terrorists attempt to bomb a US-bound airliner?

2. How many Joint Terrorism Task Forces (JTTFs) does Comey say there are across the United States?

3. How many industry partners does the FBI work with at the National Cyber-Forensics and Training Alliance, according to Comey?

Today's FBI [Federal Bureau of Investigation] is a threat-focused, intelligence-driven organization. Every FBI professional understands that preventing the key threats facing our nation means constantly striving to be more efficient and more effective.

Just as our adversaries continue to evolve, so, too, must the FBI. We live in a time of acute and persistent terrorist and criminal threats to our national security, our economy, and to our communities.

These diverse threats illustrate the complexity and breadth of the FBI's mission and make clear the importance of its partnerships. We cannot do it alone. To accomplish its mission, the FBI relies heavily upon its partners around the globe.

In fact, our national headquarters and local field offices have built partnerships with just about every federal, state, local, tribal, and territorial law enforcement agency in the nation. Our agents and professional staff also work closely with law enforcement, intelligence, and security services in foreign countries, as well as international organizations like INTERPOL [International Criminal Police Organization].

By combining our resources and leveraging our collective expertise, we are able to investigate national security threats that cross both geographical and jurisdictional boundaries.

It is important to emphasize that the FBI carries out this broad mission with rigorous obedience to the rule of law and protecting the civil rights and civil liberties of the citizens we serve.

Counterterrorism

Counterterrorism remains our top priority. The FBI works with our law enforcement and intelligence community (IC) partners to integrate intelligence and operations and to detect and disrupt terrorists and their organizations.

As the Boston bombings this past April [2013] illustrate, the terrorist threat against the United States remains very real. We face a continuing threat from homegrown extremists, especially those who act alone or in small cells. Homegrown violent extremists (HVEs) present unique challenges because they do not share a typical profile and their experiences and motives are often distinct, which makes them difficult to identify and their plots difficult to disrupt. Al Qaeda and its affiliates continue to encourage extremists in the West to follow this model by engaging in individual violent attacks and have already incorporated the Boston bombings in their propaganda. The Boston Marathon bombing suspects are from the North Caucasus, but the links, if any, between the bombing and that region remain unclear. We currently assess the threat from North Caucasus–based militants to the homeland to be minimal as they remain focused on fighting against Russian security forces in the North Caucasus.

The Boston bombing also demonstrated the devastating potential of an improvised explosive device (IED) crafted from simple components, which could inspire other extremists to use such tactics. The devices used in Boston were similar in design to instructions widely available online. In addition to the Boston attack, over the past two years we have also seen extremists attempt to detonate IEDs or bombs at such high-profile targets as the Federal Reserve Bank in New York, the U.S. Capitol, and commercial establishments in downtown Chicago, Tampa, and Oakland. Fortunately, these attempts, as well as many other plots, were thwarted. Yet the threat remains.

Overseas, the terrorist threat is similarly complex and ever changing. We are seeing more groups engaged in terrorism, a wider array of terrorist targets, greater cooperation among terrorist groups, and continued evolution and adaptation in tactics and communication. Al Qaeda and its affiliates, especially al Qaeda in the Arabian Peninsula (AQAP), continue to represent a top terrorist threat to the nation. These groups have attempted several attacks on the United States, including the failed Christmas Day airliner bombing in 2009, the attempted bombing of U.S.-bound cargo planes in October of 2010, and a disrupted plot to conduct a suicide bomb attack on a U.S.-bound airliner in April 2012.

Threats from Africa

Beyond the Middle East, threats emanating from Africa remain a concern to the FBI. Al-Shabaab, based in Somalia, recently attacked the Westgate mall in Nairobi, Kenya. The FBI continues to assess that al-Shabaab lacks the intent to conduct or directly support attacks in the United States, as doing so would not be consistent with the group's strategic aims of establishing an Islamic state in Somalia and defeating the Somali and foreign troops obstructing their efforts to do so. We expect Kenya to remain the primary focus of the group's external attacks, though other nearby countries participating in military offensives against the group, such as Ethiopia and Uganda, remain at risk as well. Nonetheless, the FBI remains concerned that externally focused elements affiliated with the group are likely to aspire to attack the West and the U.S. Additionally, domestic extremists could draw inspiration from the group's propaganda and the Westgate mall attack to employ similar tactics in the homeland.

In North Africa, al Qaeda in the Lands of the Islamic Maghreb (AQIM) continues to grow its operational reach and safe haven into Libya and Mali, threatening U.S. and Western interests in the region. The FBI assesses AQIM, its affiliates and allies, and aspirant groups in the region pose a low threat to the homeland in the short to mid term, but pose a high threat to U.S. and Western interests in the region, especially at embassies, hotels, and diplomatic facilities in Tunisia and Libya. Since 2009, AQIM has a demonstrated capability to target Western interests, most notably through kidnap for ransom techniques. Since 2011, AQIM splinter groups, along with Libya- and Tunisia-based Ansar al-Sharia extremists, have increasingly proven their anti-Western ideologies through high-profile attacks on the U.S. consulate in Benghazi, Libya; the U.S. embassy in Tunis, Tunisia; British oil facilities in Algeria; and a French-owned mine in Arlit, Niger. Such attacks against U.S. interests will likely continue, especially as extremists continue to fight for autonomy and control against governments which they perceive are receiving assistance from the United States.

With respect to West Africa, the FBI assesses that Nigeria-based Boko Haram does not currently pose a threat to the homeland. Boko Haram does, however, aspire to attack U.S. or Western interests in the region. Boko Haram demonstrated its capability for such attacks in its 2011 vehicle-borne IED attack on the United Nations headquarters in Abuja, Nigeria. Current counterterrorism pressure from Nigerian military and police forces has limited Boko Haram's ability to execute various operational plans against Western targets; however, communications, training, and weapons links between Boko Haram and AQIM, al-Shabaab, and AQAP may strengthen

Boko Haram's capacity to conduct terrorist attacks against U.S. or Western targets in the future.

Confronting Terrorist Threats

To combat these threats, the FBI relies upon its 103 Joint Terrorism Task Forces (JTTFs) across the nation and 63 legal attaché (legat) offices around the world. The FBI has added approximately 70 JTTFs since 9/11 [referring to the September 11, 2001, terrorist attacks on the United States]. Investigators, analysts, linguists, and SWAT experts from dozens of U.S. law enforcement and intelligence agencies comprise the JTTFs. The JTTFs serve as critical force multipliers that follow up on all terrorism leads, develop and investigate cases, and proactively identify threats and trends that may impact the region, the nation, and the world.

Since 9/11, JTTFs have been instrumental in breaking up cells like the Portland Seven, the Northern Virginia jihad group, and the Daniel Patrick Boyd cell in North Carolina. They've foiled attacks against military institutions and personnel in New Jersey, New York, Maryland, Washington, Texas, and Virginia. They have disrupted plots against government and civilian targets across the country, including the al Qaeda plot against the New York City subway in 2009. They have traced sources of terrorist funding, responded to anthrax and other suspected weapons of mass destruction threats, halted the use of fake IDs, and arrested subjects who possessed deadly weapons and explosives.

To better address the evolving threat, the FBI has also established the Countering Violent Extremism (CVE) office. This office leverages FBI resources and works with federal counterparts to empower our local partners to prevent violent extremists and their supporters from inspiring, radicalizing, financing, or recruiting individuals or groups in the United States to commit acts of violence. The FBI is leading efforts to conduct outreach and raise community awareness while up-holding civil rights and liberties.

Cyber Threats

The diverse threats we face are increasingly cyber based. Much of America's most sensitive data is stored on computers. We are losing data, money, and ideas through cyber intrusions. This threatens innovation and, as citizens, we are also increasingly vulnerable to losing our personal information. That is why we anticipate that in the future, resources devoted to cyber-based threats will equal or even eclipse the resources devoted to non-cyber-based terrorist threats.

The FBI has built up substantial expertise to address cyber threats, both in the homeland and overseas.

Here at home, the FBI serves as the executive agent for the National Cyber Investigative Joint Task Force (NCIJTF) which joins together 19 intelligence, law enforcement, and military agencies to coordinate cyber-threat investigations. The FBI works closely with all our partners in the NCIJTF, including the National Security Agency (NSA) and the Department of Homeland Security (DHS). We have different responsibilities, but we must work together on cyber-threat investigations to the extent of our authorities and share information among the three of us, following the principle that notification of an intrusion to one agency will be notification to all.

While national-level coordination is important to securing the nation, teamwork at the local level is also essential. After more than a decade of combating cybercrime through a nationwide network of interagency task forces, the FBI has evolved its Cyber Task Forces (CTFs) in all 56 field offices to focus exclusively on cybersecurity threats. In addition to key law enforcement and homeland security agencies at the state and local level, each CTF partners with many of the federal agencies that participate in the NCIJTF at the headquarters level. This promotes effective collaboration and de-confliction of efforts at both the local and national level.

Through the FBI's legal attaché offices around the globe and partnerships with our international counterparts, we are sharing information and coordinating cyber investigations more than ever. We have special agents working alongside our foreign police department partners; they work to identify emerging trends and key players in the cybercrime arena.

It is important to note that we are also coordinating closely with our federal partners on the policy that drives our investigative efforts. Although our agencies have different roles, we also understand that we must work together on every significant intrusion and to share information among the three of us, following the principle that notification of an intrusion to one agency will be notification to all.

The Role of the Private Sector

In addition to cooperation within the government, there must be cooperation with the private sector. The private sector is the key player in cybersecurity. Private sector companies are the primary victims of cyber intrusions. And they also possess the information, the expertise, and the knowledge to address cyber intrusions and cybercrime in general. In February 2013, the Bureau held the first session of our National Cyber Executive Institute, a three-day seminar to train leading industry executives on cyber-threat awareness and information sharing.

One example of an effective public-private partnership is the National Cyber-Forensics and Training Alliance, a proven model for sharing private sector information in collaboration with law enforcement. Located in Pittsburgh, the alliance includes more than 80 industry partners from a range of sectors, including financial services, telecommunications, retail and manufacturing. The members of the alliance work together with federal and international partners to provide real-time threat intelligence, every day.

Another initiative the FBI participates in, the Enduring Security Framework, includes top leaders from the private sector and the federal government. This partnership illustrates that the way forward on cybersecurity is not just about sharing information, but also about solving problems together.

We intend to build more bridges to the private sector in the cybersecurity realm. We must fuse private sector information with information from the intelligence community and develop channels for sharing information and intelligence quickly and effectively.

Operation Clean Slate

In the last several years, the distribution of malicious software through networks of infected computers, or botnets, by online criminals has emerged as a global cybersecurity threat. As a response, the FBI developed Operation Clean Slate, a broad team effort to address this significant threat. Operation Clean Slate is the FBI's comprehensive public-private approach to eliminate the most significant botnet activity and increase the practical consequences for those who use botnets for intellectual property theft or other criminal activities.

In April 2013, the FBI implemented this plan and identified the Citadel botnet as the highest priority botnet threat. Citadel is a type of malware known as a banking trojan. This type of malicious software is designed to facilitate unauthorized access to computers to steal online banking credentials, credit card information, and other personally identifiable information (PII).

Focusing on the Citadel malware, Operation Clean Slate identified the specific actors: the coders who create the botnet, the herders who aggregate victim computers, and the users who utilize the botnet. We also identified intended or actual victims of the botnet.

The FBI and its global partners then took action against Citadel. Through court-ordered authorizations and leveraging industry partnerships, more than 1,400 controlling components of the botnet were disrupted, essentially ceasing its operations. Once these controlling components were rendered inoperable, it is estimated Operation Clean Slate freed more than 2.1 million robot computers from this malicious network.

The FBI must continue to develop and deploy creative solutions in order to defeat today's complex cyber-threat actors. Instead of just building better defenses, we must also build better relationships, overcoming the obstacles that prevent us from sharing information and, most importantly, collaborating.

Active-Shooter Threats

The recent shootings at the Navy Yard in Washington, D.C., the Los Angeles [International] Airport, and the Westfield Garden State Plaza mall demonstrate that communities across America continue to face active shooter and mass casualty incidents. Since the Sandy Hook tragedy last December, the FBI has been working with the Department of Justice's [DOJ's] Bureau of Justice Assistance to provide tactical active-shooter training to law enforcement agencies across the country. In conjunction with this training, the FBI and DOJ, working with our HHS [Department of Health and Human Services], Education, and DHS partners, have developed an active-shooter brochure and planning guides to complement this effort.

Over the past year, 100 FBI agents have attended the Advanced Law Enforcement Rapid Response Training (ALERRT) school and trained other officers in lifesaving tactics. The 16-hour basic active-shooter course prepares first responders to isolate a threat, distract the threat actors, and end the threat. In addition, during the month of April, the FBI conducted two-day conferences and tabletop exercises with state, local, tribal, and campus law enforcement executives. The purpose of these conferences was to ensure that the ALERRT brought FBI field offices and law enforcement command staff together to discuss best practices and lessons learned from mass shooting incidents. We have hosted two-day conferences on active-shooter situations at most of our 56 field offices nationwide followed by tabletop exercises based on real-life incidents.

These incidents have also given rise to collaboration among behavioral experts, victim assistance specialists, and other personnel to work through best practices, including how to best react to active shooter and mass casualty incidents. We are continuing our efforts with a new tabletop exercise specifically designed for campus law enforcement. This is an issue that impacts all of us, and the FBI is committed to working with our partners to protect our communities.

> "The key question, at least outside of war zones, is not 'are we safer?' but 'how safe are we?'"

The Terrorist Threat Has Been Exaggerated

John Mueller

John Mueller is an author, political and security analyst, and professor at the Ohio State University. In the following viewpoint, he asserts that the terrorist threat to the United States is real and credible but is much more narrow and limited than the media and government officials make it. Mueller argues that it is often exaggerated by implying links and connections between disparate terrorist groups or hyping a terrorist group's importance or effectiveness. When judging the effectiveness of terrorist acts, Mueller explains that the evidence shows that mass shooters have done more damage within the United States. He argues that Americans are really quite safe from terrorism; in fact, statistics show that Americans are in more danger of becoming a homicide victim or dying from cancer than being a victim of a terrorist attack.

As you read, consider the following questions:

1. According to Mueller, what group do terrorism alarmists call the deadliest and most aggressive of al Qaeda's affiliates?

2. How many people does the author report have been killed by Islamist terrorists in the United States in the years since 2001?

3. What is the chance of an American becoming a victim of terrorism in the United States, according to the author?

Two years after the raid on Osama bin Laden's hideaway, terrorism alarmists remain in peak form explaining that although al-Qaeda has been weakened it still manages to present a grave threat.

Various well-honed techniques are applied to support this contention. One is to espy and assess various "linkages" or "connections" of "ties" or "threads" between and among a range of disparate terrorists or terrorist groups, most of which appear rather gossamer and of only limited consequence on closer examination.

Another is to exaggerate the importance and effectiveness of the "affiliated groups" linked to al-Qaeda central. In particular, alarmists point to the al-Qaeda affiliate in chaotic Yemen, ominously hailing it as the "deadliest" and the "most aggressive" of these and a "major threat."

Yet its chief efforts at international terrorism have failed abysmally: an underwear bomb and laser printer bombs on cargo planes. With that track record, the group may pose a problem or concern, but it scarcely presents a "major threat" outside of war zones.

A Diminishing Threat?

More generally, "al-Qaeda is its own worst enemy," as Robert Grenier, a former top CIA [Central Intelligence Agency] counterterrorism official, notes. "Where they have succeeded initially, they very quickly discredit themselves."

Any terrorist threat within the developed world seems even less impressive. The Boston terrorists of 2013 were the first in the United States since 9/11 [referring to the September 11, 2001, terrorist attacks on the United States] in which Islamist terrorists actually were able to assemble and detonate bombs—albeit very primitive ones. But except for that, they do not seem to have been more competent than most of their predecessors.

Amazingly, they apparently thought they could somehow get away with their deed even though they chose to set their bombs off at the most-photographed spot on the planet at the time. Moreover, they had no coherent plan of escape and, as commonly found, no ability to explain how killing a few random people would advance their cause.

While the scope of the tragedy in Boston should not be minimized, it should also be noted that if the terrorists' aim was to kill a large number of people, their bombs failed miserably. As recent cases [of mass shootings] in Colorado and Connecticut sadly demonstrate, far more fatalities have been inflicted by gunmen.

Before Boston, some 16 people had been killed by Islamist terrorists in the United States in the years since 2001, and all of these were murdered by people who were essentially acting alone. By contrast, in the 1970s, organized terrorists inflicted hundreds of attacks, mostly bombings, in the United States, killing 72.

The Danger of Lone-Wolf Attacks

As concern about organized attacks has diminished, fear of "lone wolf" attacks has grown in recent years, and one official assessment contends that "lone offenders currently present the greatest threat."

"WE'D LIKE TO VISIT A PEACEFUL POLICE STATE AWAY FROM ANY TERROR THREATS."

© Harley Schwardron/Cartoonstock.com.

This is a reasonable observation, but those concerned should keep in mind that, as analyst Max Abrahms has noted, while lone wolves may be difficult to police, they have carried out only two of the 1,900 most deadly terrorist attacks over the last four decades.

The Real Question

The key question, at least outside of war zones, is not "are we safer?" but "how safe are we?"

At current rates, an American's chance of becoming a victim of terrorism in the U.S., even with 9/11 in the calculation, is about 1 in 3.5 million per year. In comparison, that same American stands a 1 in 22,000 yearly chance of becoming a homicide victim, a 1 in 8,000 chance of perishing in an auto accident, and a 1 in 500 chance of dying from cancer.

These calculations are based, of course, on historical data. However, alarmists who would reject such history need to explain why they think terrorists will suddenly become vastly more competent in the future.

But no one seems to be making that argument. Indeed, notes one reporter, U.S. officials now say that al-Qaeda has become less capable of a large attack like 9/11. But she also says that they made this disclosure only on condition of anonymity out of fear that "publicly identifying themselves could make them a target" of terrorists.

In contrast, one terrorism specialist, Peter Bergen, has observed in heroic full attribution mode that, "The last terror attack (in the West) was seven years ago in London," that there "haven't been any major attacks in the U.S.," and that "they are recruiting no-hopers and dead-enders."

Terrorists do, of course, exist—as they have throughout history. They may even get lucky again sometime. Thus, concern and watchfulness about terrorism is justified. But counterterrorism expenditures that are wildly disproportionate to the limited hazard terrorism presents are neither wise nor responsible.

> "While there are a number of critical is-
> sues involving the world's water re-
> sources, we have to make solving the
> global water crisis for the men, women,
> and children living and dying its daily
> reality a central priority."

The Declining Access to Potable Water Will Lead to Global Instability

Gary White

*Gary White is the chief executive officer of Water.org. In the fol-
lowing viewpoint, he identifies ending global water poverty as an
issue worthy of more attention and resources. One reason is that
there are too many deaths caused by water-related disease in the
world. Another is that a lack of safe water is regarded as a global
security threat, causing instability in developing nations because
of its scarcity. White says that providing safe water is essential to
protect health and ensure security and is a key factor in economic development. He explains that there have been a number
of pioneering initiatives to tackle the problem.*

As you read, consider the following questions:

1. According to White, what percentage of the world's water is used for agriculture?

2. How many children under the age of five does the author report will die every twenty seconds because of a preventable water-related disease?

3. According to the author's estimations, how many people in India will receive access to safe water or improved sanitation by 2016 through WaterCredit?

This [Is water the world's next global security threat?] was the question posed last weekend at the 2012, Aspen Ideas Festival. I was pleased to see the topic discussed in earnest, not just on day five, but throughout the week. I say this because I find the topic of ensuring access to safe water and sanitation for the world's poor rarely gets this level of attention. It's a welcome shift! Don't get me wrong. Important issues such as food security, energy, nutrition, culture, and political stability all merit equal attention, but like a fractal design, the center depends on the vantage point. For me, and Water.org, it's achieving this ambitious goal—ending global water poverty as we know it. It's our focus because water, for being one of the most abundant and elemental resources on the planet, isn't available to nearly a billion people. Furthermore, more people on the planet have access to a cell phone than to a toilet.

Often, when we focus our attention on water, we find the conversation turns to very broad and interrelated challenges, which can quickly become so complex it's hard to remember where you began. Let's first confirm that there is indeed enough water on the planet to sustain each living person. While it's true that population growth continues to apply increasing pressure on water resources, the reality is that only 8% of the world's water use is for households. About 70% of

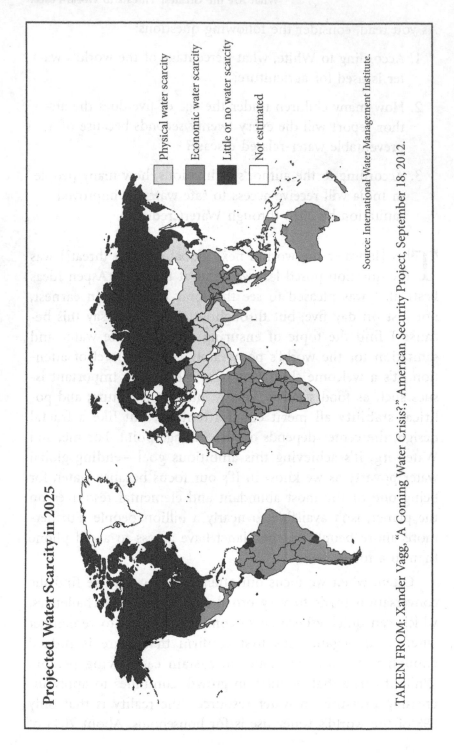

Projected Water Scarcity in 2025

Physical water scarcity

Economic water scarcity

Little or no water scarcity

Not estimated

Source: International Water Management Institute.

TAKEN FROM: Xander Vagg, "A Coming Water Crisis?," American Security Project, September 18, 2012.

all water on the planet is used for agriculture. If every single person in the world without access to safe water secured 50 liters for basic daily use, it would take a mere fraction of 1% of the world's water resources (by comparison, the per capita use in the United States is more than 350 liters).

Safe Water

Assuming we have enough water, we can now focus on safe water. A child under the age of five will die from a preventable water-related disease before you finish reading this paragraph. That's a child every 20 seconds, every day.

While there are a number of critical issues involving the world's water resources, we have to make solving the global water crisis for the men, women, and children living and dying its daily reality a central priority. Solutions to large-scale water use and management challenges are in development, yet the world is divided—in developed countries there is looming anxiety about water shortages, whereas in developing nations it is a real and deadly certainty. There are more children dying of preventable, water- and sanitation-related disease than HIV/AIDS and malaria combined. Women across the world spend millions of hours a day collecting water for their families and often that water is contaminated by animal and human waste. The choice between dying of dehydration or water-related illness is made every single day. For those living in informal settlements, access to water comes at a high price—often 5–10 times more per liter of water than their middle-upper-class neighbors with house connections living in the same city.

Besides ensuring basic survival for nearly a billion people, universal access to safe water will increase global security and, according to the World Health Organization, will give an economic return of $3 to $34 dollars for every dollar invested. The good news is that this challenge doesn't require us to wait for a miracle cure. The world has been able to deliver safe water and basic sanitation for more than 100 years. Imagine if we cured cancer or HIV/AIDS and 4,000 children died every day because we failed to deliver the cure. We simply would not stand for it.

New Initiatives

One of the central themes during the festival was the power of collaborations between sometimes unsuspecting partners to tackle some of the world's most pressing problems—like ending the global water crisis. One such partner is PepsiCo. They're focused on a Recipe for the Next Billion and how they will meet the needs of the next billion; doing more while using less. As a global food and beverage company, water is fundamental to PepsiCo's ability to operate and they have been committed to finding ways to sustain and protect the world's water resources. And so our worlds intersect.

In partnership with the PepsiCo Foundation, Water.org will provide access to safe water or improved sanitation to nearly 1 million people in India by 2016 through an innovative approach called WaterCredit. WaterCredit is a market-driven model that Water.org pioneered in 2003 where microfinance institutions (MFIs) provide small (micro) loans to individuals to finance their own water and sanitation solutions, such as rainwater harvesting tanks, a toilet, or a household connection to a water utility. To date, more than 187,000 people in India have benefitted from improved water and sanitation from this program and global repayment rates for WaterCredit are 97%. There will never be enough charity in the world to solve the global water crisis, so we need to double down on smart solutions like WaterCredit which can rapidly scale safe water and sanitation access for families that are in desperate need right now.

Ideas like WaterCredit are born from cross-pollinating innovation—in this case microfinance and water and PepsiCo and Water.org—and give us line of sight on solving the global water crisis. We are closer than ever to closing the final gap on this challenge and we will solve it with equally pioneering efforts focused on managing water resources and its equitable allocation to the poorest among us. We must remain inclusive and urgently committed to solving this for the billions who can't afford to wait.

Periodical and Internet Sources Bibliography

The following articles have been selected to supplement the diverse views presented in this chapter.

| Peter Beinart | "Why Doesn't Anyone Care About the Rising U.S.-China Tension?," *Daily Beast*, December 16, 2013. |

| David Brooks | "One Great Big War," *New York Times*, August 29, 2013. |

| Tony Burman | "Does Russia or Iran Pose Greater Danger to World Peace?," *Toronto Star*, March 22, 2014. |

| Noam Chomsky | "Why America and Israel Are the Greatest Threats to Peace," *AlterNet*, September 3, 2012. |

| David Cronin | "Forget Iran—Israel Is Bigger Threat to World Peace," *New Europe*, April 1, 2012. |

| Jason Fekete | "Iran Is the 'World's Most Serious Threat to International Peace': Stephen Harper," *National Post*, January 5, 2012. |

| Suzanne Goldenberg | "Why Global Water Shortages Pose Threat of Terror and War," *Guardian*, February 8, 2014. |

| Alexander J. Motyl | "The Dangers of the Putin Doctrine," *Al Jazeera America*, March 5, 2014. |

| Chandran Nair | "Why Is the West Seen as the Greatest Threat? From Asia, the Answer's Clear," *Guardian*, March 6, 2014. |

| Bruce Schneier | "It's Smart Politics to Exaggerate Terrorist Threats," *CNN*, May 20, 2013. |

| Sarah Wolfe | "4 Biggest Threats to Global Peace: Guess Who's No. 1?," *Salon.com*, January 9, 2014. |

For Further Discussion

Chapter 1

1. Alex Lickerman argues that world peace is possible if people transform themselves. Conversely, Aung San Suu Kyi claims that world peace is unattainable because of the negative forces in society. With which author do you agree, and why?

2. According to Miles Taylor, the concept of world peace in formulating foreign policy is immoral and dangerous. What are the author's main arguments in the viewpoint? Do you agree with Taylor? Explain your reasoning.

3. Kim R. Holmes attacks the national security strategy of the Barack Obama administration. What problems does Holmes see with the administration's strategy? Do you agree with Holmes? Why, or why not?

Chapter 2

1. Margaret MacMillan maintains that an international order can secure world peace. In your opinion, does the author provide sufficient evidence to support her claim? Why, or why not?

2. Mark P. Lagon asserts that democracy brings about peace and prosperity. Do you believe the world would be more peaceful and prosperous if democracy spread throughout the world? Explain your reasoning.

3. President Barack Obama emphasizes the United States' leadership role in creating a more peaceful world. In what ways does Obama say the country will accomplish this mission? Do you think the United States has a responsibility to secure world peace? Explain your answer.

Chapter 3

1. Valerie Norville argues that women play a vital role in building durable peace and maintaining security throughout the world. Do you agree with Norville's argument? Why, or why not?

2. Hannah Wright contends that gender equality and peace are closely linked. Based on the author's arguments, do you believe a correlation exists between the two? Explain your reasoning.

3. According to the Dalai Lama, a more peaceful world is possible if individuals focus on finding inner peace. Based on the Dalai Lama's arguments, do you believe that inner peace can lead to global harmony? Explain.

Chapter 4

1. Mona Charen claims that President Barack Obama has had a weak response to recent foreign policy issues. According to Charen, how has this impacted the world? Do you agree with the author? Explain your answer.

2. James B. Comey asserts that terrorism is a serious threat to the United States and the rest of the world. On the other hand, John Mueller argues that the threat from terrorism is exaggerated. With which author do you agree, and why? Present examples from the viewpoints to support your answer.

3. Gary White maintains that a lack of safe water poses a global security threat. What evidence does White provide to support his argument? Do you agree with White's argument? Explain.

Organizations to Contact

The editors have compiled the following list of organizations concerned with the issues debated in this book. The descriptions are derived from materials provided by the organizations. All have publications or information available for interested readers. The list was compiled on the date of publication of the present volume; the information provided here may change. Be aware that many organizations take several weeks or longer to respond to inquiries, so allow as much time as possible.

Carnegie Endowment for International Peace

1779 Massachusetts Avenue NW
Washington, DC 20036-2103
(202) 483-7600 • fax: (202) 483-1840
website: carnegieendowment.org

The Carnegie Endowment for International Peace is a global network of policy research centers that seek to advance the cause of peace. With offices in the United States, Russia, China, Europe, and the Middle East, the organization analyzes and develops policy ideas related to peace and collaborates with decision makers in government, business, and civil society. Its areas of focus include climate and energy, democracy and human rights, foreign policy, and global governance, and how these issues relate to lasting world peace. Its website offers articles such as "Corruption: The Unrecognized Threat to International Security" and "Peace on Earth (Well, in Europe Anyway)."

Carter Center

One Copenhill, 453 Freedom Parkway, Atlanta, GA 30307
(404) 420-5100
e-mail: carterweb@emory.edu
website: www.cartercenter.org

In partnership with Emory University, the Carter Center is a nongovernmental organization dedicated to human rights and the alleviation of human suffering. The center believes that a culture of respect for human rights is crucial to permanent world peace. To that end, the organization works to resolve conflicts, enhance freedom and democracy, and improve health. Its peace programs strengthen freedom and democracy in nations worldwide, securing for people the political and civil rights that are the foundation of just and peaceful societies. The Carter Center publishes the newsletter *Carter Center News*, and its website offers information on its various peace programs.

Center for International Policy (CIP)
2000 M Street NW, Suite 720, Washington, DC   20036
(202) 232-3317 • fax: (202) 232-3340
e-mail: cip@ciponline.org
website: www.ciponline.org

The Center for International Policy (CIP) is a nonprofit organization founded in 1975. Headquartered in Washington, DC, CIP supports efforts to increase transparency in foreign policy and to promote peace, democracy, demilitarization, and human rights. CIP's website offers various publications, including the reports "A Sustainable, Just, and Peaceful World" and "Report to Supporters: Addressing Challenges to Global Security."

Council on Foreign Relations (CFR)
The Harold Pratt House, 58 East Sixty-Eighth Street
New York, NY   10065
(212) 434-9400 • fax: (212) 434-9800
e-mail: communications@cfr.org
website: www.cfr.org

The Council on Foreign Relations (CFR) is an independent, nonpartisan membership organization, think tank, and publisher. CFR is home to more than seventy full-time, adjunct, and visiting scholars and practitioners who cover the world's major regions as well as the critical issues shaping today's global agenda, including the issue of world peace. The Peace, Conflict and Human Rights section of the CFR website includes the topic of peacekeeping with articles, op-eds, transcripts, and audio and video presentations on the topic. In addition, CFR publishes the magazine *Foreign Affairs*, which features articles such as "Drop Your Weapons" and "Keep Hope Alive."

Hoover Institution

434 Galvez Mall, Stanford University
Stanford, CA 94305-6010
(650) 723-1754
website: www.hoover.org

The Hoover Institution is a public policy research center focused on improving the human condition by promoting economic opportunity and prosperity and securing and safeguarding peace for the United States and the rest of the world. Located at Stanford University, the institution features renowned scholars and a library and archives. Available on its website are the publications *Hoover Daily Report, Hoover Digest*, and *Defining Ideas*, which feature articles such as "How Peace Gets Made" and "Keeping the Peace."

Institute for Economics and Peace (IEP)

3 East Fifty-Fourth Street, 14th Floor
New York, New York 10022
(646) 963-2160
website: economicsandpeace.org

The Institute for Economics and Peace (IEP) is a nonprofit think tank that seeks to focus the world's attention on "peace as a positive, achievable, and tangible measure of human well-being and progress." Among other duties, the organization develops new conceptual frameworks to define peacefulness, provides metrics for measurement, and identifies the relationship between peace, business, and prosperity. IEP publishes papers, policy recommendations, and reports, including the "2014 Global Peace Index Report" and "Pillars of Peace."

Nuclear Age Peace Foundation (NAPF)

1622 Anacapa Street, Santa Barbara, CA 93101
(805) 965-3443
website: www.wagingpeace.org

Founded in 1982, the Nuclear Age Peace Foundation (NAPF) is a nonprofit, nonpartisan organization that advocates peace and a world free of nuclear weapons. The organization consists of more than sixty thousand individuals and groups worldwide and has consultative status with the United Nations. NAPF publishes the e-newsletter the *Sunflower*, which includes the articles "War Makes Us Poorer" and "Latin American and Caribbean Nations Proclaim Zone of Peace."

Peace Action

Montgomery Center, 8630 Fenton Street, Suite 524
Silver Spring, MD 20910
(301) 565-4050 • fax: (301) 565-0850
e-mail: info@peace-action.org
website: www.peace-action.org

Peace Action is a national grassroots peace network that seeks to influence the US Congress and administration through a concerted effort of its national chapters and affiliates. By writing to the government, engaging in Internet and direct actions, and lobbying citizens, the organization attempts to promote peace legislation within the US government. The group's current antiwar issues include nuclear disarmament. Details about the background of this initiative and current actions being taken can be found on Peace Action's website, including the article "Organizing for a World Free from Nuclear Weapons."

Peace Alliance

1616 P Street NW, Suite 100, Washington, DC 20036
(202) 684-2553 • fax: (202) 204-5712
e-mail: info@thepeacealliance.org
website: peacealliance.org

The Peace Alliance is a nonprofit organization that works to empower civic engagement toward a culture of peace. With grassroots teams of volunteers throughout the United States, the organization advocates peace-building legislation and policies, educates the public and political leaders about peace building, and supports individuals and groups working for political change. The Peace Alliance's website provides numerous publications, including "The Leading Edge of Peace: Our Evolutionary Path Forward" and "Preventing Mass Atrocities: An Agenda for Policymakers and Citizens."

United States Institute of Peace (USIP)

2301 Constitution Avenue NW, Washington, DC 20037
(202) 457-1700
website: www.usip.org

The United States Institute of Peace (USIP) is an independent conflict-management center tasked by the US Congress with finding peaceful methods to mitigate international conflicts. USIP strives "to save lives, increase the government's ability to deal with conflicts before they escalate, reduce government costs, and enhance our national security." USIP produces a number of publications, including *PeaceBriefs*, *PeaceWorks*, and *Special Reports*. Its website features articles such as "Holding It Together" and reports such as "Countering Violent Extremism: A Peacebuilding Perspective."

Women's International League for Peace and Freedom (WILPF)

777 UN Plaza, 6th Floor, New York, NY 10017
(212) 682-1265 • fax: (212) 286-8211
website: www.wilpfinternational.org

Established in 1915, the Women's International League for Peace and Freedom (WILPF) is a nongovernmental organization that brings together women throughout the world who work for peace and promote political, economic, and social justice. The organization has consultation status with the United Nations. The organization's PeaceWomen Programme was started in 2000 to ensure that women's rights and participation are not disregarded in international peace and security efforts. Its "Women, Peace, and Security Handbook" offers recommendations on incorporating gender and women's rights into the work of the United Nations peacekeeping efforts. WILPF publishes various newsletters, articles, and reports, which are available on its website.

World Policy Institute (WPI)
108 West Thirty-Ninth Street, Suite 1000
New York, NY   10018
(212) 481-5005 • fax: (212) 481-5009
e-mail: wpi@worldpolicy.org
website: www.worldpolicy.org

The World Policy Institute (WPI) has been working for half a century to provide trusted nonpartisan and international policy leadership. The institute's goal is to ensure a stable global market economy open to all, to foster informed global civic participation to create effective governments, and to encourage international cooperation on national and global security issues. WPI's website offers the *World Policy Blog*, which features numerous articles on world peace, including "Could a New US Strategy Bring Peace?"

Bibliography of Books

Thorsten Benner, Stephan Mergenthaler, and Philipp Rotmann
The New World of UN Peace Operations: Learning to Build Peace? New York: Oxford University Press, 2011.

Jalaja Bonheim
Evolving Toward Peace: Awakening the Global Heart. Minneapolis, MN: Two Harbors Press, 2013.

Stephen L. Carter
The Violence of Peace: America's Wars in the Age of Obama. New York: Beast Books, 2011.

Paul K. Chappell
The Art of Waging Peace: A Strategic Approach to Improving Our Lives and the World. Westport, CT: Prospecta Press, 2013.

Paul K. Chappell
Peaceful Revolution: How We Can Create the Future Needed for Humanity's Survival. Westport, CT: Easton Studio Press, 2012.

Ron Clasky
An Alternate Vision: For a Peaceful World. Seattle, WA: CreateSpace, 2012.

Roland Dannreuther
International Security: The Contemporary Agenda. Malden, MA: Polity Press, 2013.

Bruce W. Dayton and Louis Kriesberg, eds.
Conflict Transformation and Peacebuilding: Moving from Violence to Sustainable Peace. New York: Routledge, 2009.

Paul F. Diehl and Alexandru Balas — *Peace Operations*. Malden, MA: Polity Press, 2014.

Paul F. Diehl and Brian Frederking, eds. — *The Politics of Global Governance: International Organizations in an Interdependent World*. Boulder, CO: Lynne Rienner Publishers, 2010.

Valerie M. Hudson, Bonnie Ballif-Spanvill, Mary Caprioli, and Chad F. Emmett — *Sex and World Peace*. New York: Columbia University Press, 2012.

Brent N. Hunter — *The Rainbow Bridge: Bridge to Inner Peace and to World Peace*. 4th ed. San Francisco, CA: Spirit Rising Productions, 2014.

Margaret P. Karns and Karen A. Mingst — *International Organizations: The Politics and Processes of Global Governance*. Boulder, CO: Lynne Rienner Publishers, 2009.

Louis Kriesberg and Bruce W. Dayton — *Constructive Conflicts: From Escalation to Resolution*. Lanham, MD: Rowman & Littlefield, 2012.

Bruce Bueno de Mesquita — *Principles of International Politics: War, Peace, and World Order*. Thousand Oaks, CA: CQ Press, 2014.

Seyed Hossein Mousavian with Shahir Shahidsaless — *Iran and the United States: An Insider's View on the Failed Past and the Road to Peace*. New York: Bloomsbury, 2014.

Rob Noyes-Smith *Revolution Without Violence: An Ordinary Man's Guide to Peace and Prosperity in a Dangerous World.* Litchfield Park, AZ: Emergent Publications, 2012.

Felix M. Padilla *The Struggle for the Authentic Self: Creating Your True Self for a Peaceful World.* The Woodlands, TX: Indigo Heart Publishing, 2010.

Malcolm Potts and Thomas Hayden *Sex and War: How Biology Explains Warfare and Terrorism and Offers a Path to a Safer World.* Dallas, TX: BenBella Books, 2010.

David E. Sanger *Confront and Conceal: Obama's Secret Wars and Surprising Use of American Power.* New York: Crown Publishers, 2012.

Scott R. Sernau *Global Problems: The Search for Equity, Peace, and Sustainability.* New York: Pearson, 2012.

Michael E. Smith *International Security: Politics, Policy, Prospects.* New York: Palgrave Macmillan, 2010.

Jonathan Tonge *Comparative Peace Processes.* Malden, MA: Polity Press, 2014.

Charles P. Webel and Jørgen Johansen, eds. *Peace and Conflict Studies: A Reader.* New York: Routledge, 2011.

Thomas G. Weiss, *The United Nations and Changing*
David P. Forsythe, *World Politics.* 7th ed. Boulder, CO:
Roger A. Coate, Westview Press, 2013.
and Kelly-Kate
Pease

Index

A

Abbas, Mahmoud, 15
Abductions
    Lord's Resistance Army
        (Uganda), 119–120, 123
    West Bank, 14–15
    women, 143–144
Abrahms, Max, 208
Abu Khdeir, Mohammed, 15
"Accidental" causes of war, 69,
    70–71, 73
Active shooter threats, 203–204
Adorney, Julian, 110–115
Advanced Law Enforcement Rapid
    Response Training (ALERRT),
    203–204
Afghanistan
    Soviet invasion, 1979, 64
    terrorism and intervention-
        ism, 187
    US involvement and out-
        comes, 74, 78, 92, 105
    US military: women, 122
    women politicians, 121, 129
    women's rights and work,
        126–127
    as world's most violent na-
        tion, 72
AFL-CIO, 88
Africa
    terrorist groups, 197–199
    US foreign policy history,
        167–169
    women politicians, 120, 121,
        125
    See also specific countries
African American rights, 100
African National Congress, 168

African Union, 77–78
Aggregate trade, 114
Agriculture
    water use, 211, 213
    women's economic develop-
        ment, 120
Ahmadinejad, Mahmoud, 172–
    173, 189
Airline terrorism, 197, 206
al Qaeda
    encouragement to other ter-
        rorists, 196
    plots foiled/weakness, 199,
        206–207, 209
    structure, 93, 206
    support, 186
    Syria, 103, 104
    US fight against, 92, 93, 97
al Qaeda in the Arabian Peninsula
    (AQAP), 197, 198–199
al Qaeda in the Lands of the Is-
    lamic Maghreb (AQIM), 198
Al-Shabaab (terrorist group), 197,
    198–199
Algeria, 198
Amongi, Betty, 121, 123
Anarchy, 57
Angola, 168–169
Annan, Kofi, 89
Anthrax, 199
Apartheid, 167, 168, 169, 187
Appeasement, 42
Arab-Israeli conflict. See Israel-
    Palestine conflict
Arab nationalism, 78
Arab Spring, 58
    described, and US reactions,
        79, 86–87, 93–94